Audition *for*

Film, TV and

Commercials

with

Confidence!

The How-to Guide
to Prepare You
Before the Audition

Patrice Romero
Casting Director

How to Audition For Film, TV and Commercials with Confidence!

Copyright 2015 - Patrice Romero

ISBN: 9781520224961
Printed in the United States of AmericaFirst Edition, 2018

DEDICATION

This book is dedicated to anyone that has a desire to work in the film, TV or commercial industry. I appreciate you, the actor, as much as a good conversation, a delicious healthy organic meal, and a good romp in the hay...you get the idea. You are the reason I have been successful at building one of the largest casting companies in all of Arizona!

I dedicate this book, also, to my mother Judy who instilled strong work ethics in me at a very young age and taught me to think outside the box. To my business partner Barry who has mad computer skills and a great sense of humor and finally to my beautiful, creative and passionate daughter Taylor. She sacrificed so much to have a mom who is a very busy casting director!

About the Author

Patrice Romero
*Facilitator, organizer, entrepreneur, podcaster, social
butterfly, music lover, dancer, singer, perfectionist,
animal lover, organic foodie, vegan,*
www.onehottoddy.com *which is her goddess spirit.*

If you had to describe Patrice with just a couple of words
it would most likely be "patient", "good listener" and
"organized". Patrice also had a weird fixation with
matching people up together. This carries over into her
personal and professional life. Patrice has been
successful in introducing couples who ended up getting
married, people who become lifelong friends, as well as
matching up hundreds of actors with very grateful clients.

Patrice realizes that not every relationship will work out
though. Recently she matched up two acquaintances that
she thought would really hit it off because they were both
single and lonely, but the date turned out to be a disaster!
The female ended up being extremely unfriendly and
would not even talk to the poor guy, but the guy also had
a drinking problem that Patrice was not aware of. One
just never knows how someone will act when meeting
someone new for the first time. Despite this, Patrice is
never deterred in her enthusiasm for connecting people
together.

Patrice feels the audition process has more to do with
connecting people than acting. The clients that hire

Patrice are all looking to hire people, not actors (and certainly not alcoholics!). Casting was a perfect fit for Patrice because of this.

Growing up in Tempe Arizona, Patrice was the youngest of three girls. She was extremely shy and when younger wanted to live on a farm and be surrounded by animals. She realized after a trip to Europe that she was destined to travel and see the world. As a fluke, she interviewed with Continental Airlines and was invited to join the company right then and there, but it would require her to leave in two weeks' time for training in Houston Texas. She jumped at the opportunity! Patrice was forced to overcome her shyness due to having to make in flight announcements and handle hundreds of passengers a day.

After travelling the world for five years she found herself back in Arizona. She met her ex-husband Barry in 1993 on a photo shoot and married him five months later and they had their hilarious daughter, Taylor, the next year. Fast forward twenty years later and hundreds of credits to her name; Patrice is still busy connecting people together. She loves working with new talent and helping overcome their fear of the audition process.

While not casting, Patrice is busy singing, recording podcasts, dancing, listening to music, exercising, shopping at Whole Foods and thrift stores, cleaning and hanging out with her family and embarrassing her daughter. Check out Patrice's credits on IMDB at

http://www.imdb.com/name/nm1890066/?ref_=fn_al_nm
_1

CONTENTS

INTRODUCTION

I realized how much I enjoyed the TV/film and commercial industry after I was hired as a background extra in my mid-twenties for a couple of different television series that filmed in Arizona. I enjoyed the behind the scenes action much more than I enjoyed my time in front of the camera, so casting became the perfect fit for me. Thank goodness though for those that love being *in front* of the camera!

My indoctrination into the world of casting came about when I was asked to help cast background extras, stand ins and body doubles for a B movie filming in a small town called Globe, Arizona. It starred a handful of B actors and was very low budget. So low budget they did not have a budget to even pay me or the extras! Why, you ask would I do this? Well, I wanted *and* needed the experience. Prior to this I had only supplied promotional models to company events and tradeshows, so I gladly accepted the casting assignment.

Even though I have done this hundreds of times, I always get nervous before the audition. I am not nervous about *my* ability, but about the actors who are coming in. (Okay, I must admit that I am also worried about my ability due to the latest technology they expect us to have in place when holding auditions and as we all know technology is a blessing and a curse!). Anyway, every audition is a set of problems needing to be solved and each person walking through the door is a potential solution (or nightmare) to one of the problems. Although I cannot completely control the situation, I count on the actors to do their homework, to show up, to look presentable and to allow their personalities to come through in their audition.

Starting out, I had no idea what I was doing. I was flying by the seat of my pants, hearing industry terms I had never heard before and did not understand and speaking to industry professionals who completely intimidated me. I made *a lot* of mistakes and, believe me; my clients let me know it (behind my back usually though)! Often, I had to act like I knew what I was doing and then scramble to follow through on what I just agreed to do. It was terrifying and exhilarating at the same time!

Unfortunately, there are no coaches for casting directors. If you are lucky you can work under an experienced professional to learn the ropes; I did not have that luxury. It took time, but over the years I honed my skills, increased my experience and streamlined the process. I asked questions, researched the industry and took a pro-active approach to casting and understanding industry terms and lingo. I was also not afraid to take on low budget jobs to gain experience.

The casting industry is a team effort: without the actors, I could not do what I do. As a casting director, I want and need you to succeed! I have observed thousands of actors, over the past twenty years, in the audition process. How exciting to see actors bring the roles to life, give the characters dimension and just be themselves! I share in their enthusiasm when they land a booking. Their passion for the industry shows every time they come in.

Auditions have also allowed me to observe the frequent mistakes made by actors. Mistakes that diminish their chances of being selected or getting called back. Mistakes that make the clients whisper unkind words as the actor leaves the room. Common themes among the mistakes include: lack of "being real", lack of knowledge about the audition process, lack of preparation, lack of self-confidence, and fear.

My inexperience, starting out, allows me to relate well to these mistakes. Many times, I bit off more than I could chew. My lack of knowledge and experience showed at first, but I was determined to learn the ropes and please the clients that came to me. I learned to easily recognize these signs in actors coming to my auditions.

My career is proof that the best way to fill that void is to understand how the audition process works and to discover how you fit in. Both endeavors will lead to a more comfortable audition for you, as an actor. The audition process can become second nature to you, if you take some time to work at it and learn the process.

This guide is not about acting technique, I will leave that to your acting coach, but it *will* help you with the audition process and what to expect. You will learn practical and common-sense information, what to do and what not to do in an audition as well as how to not make a complete fool of yourself or turn off the decision makers viewing your audition.

Actors that have achieved a certain level of success have worked very hard to get there. It did not happen overnight. Be aware that the acting pool is actually very small in any given market. Meaning many casting directors bring in the same actors again and again because they know they can handle the audition process. This creates a problem for the clients though as they also like to see new faces. Actors who are positive, relaxed, prepared and believable (even in a totally unbelievable environment aka the audition room) will always stand out above those who are unprepared, self-conscious, overacting and apologetic.

Once again, I want you to succeed! When you look good, I look good! Very simply put the more that people learn how to properly handle the audition process, the more I can please my clients. The more I please my clients, the more they give us their repeat business.

While this book is geared towards a smaller market you will find that the advice I give will cross over into larger markets such as New York or Los Angeles or any other big city.

For those that may be brand new to the industry, this guide will take the mystery out of the audition process. It offers a behind-the-scenes look at the decision makers as well as how the casting process works. For those with experience auditioning, but who are not booking many jobs or getting called back, this guide will also help you to avoid common mistakes.

The good news is: anyone can learn to audition with confidence which will increase your chances of getting booked! You should see your callback ratio go up as well!

CHAPTER 1

A MULTIBILLION

DOLLAR INDUSTRY

Technology has added tremendous changes to the industry over the past 20 years. These changes have completely transformed how film and TV projects are made, as well as how commercial advertisers market their products. There is now an entire category called New Media which includes internet and mobile devices. Product websites alone are a nonstop commercial which is 24/7. Many industry professionals take advantage of this new media. Internet films, commercials and videos are a huge part of my business now. This also opens a lot of doors for new faces looking to get started in the industry!

THE REASONS FOR HIRING A CASTING DIRECTOR

Big budget projects want the best talent and are willing to pay for it; lower budget projects, after friends and family members have been recruited and then flake, are more willing to pay for a casting director's assistance. Producers know that we can put together a casting call or series of auditions and bring in the best possible talent for their project. Casting directors are known for being well connected with talent agencies and other talent resources. Some casting directors have special niches, such as real people casting (non-actors) or athletes or models. We can also provide extras or fill other nonspeaking roles, which make us indispensable to our production clients and their projects.

BUSINESS SIDE OF THE INDUSTRY

This is a multibillion dollar a year industry. Film, TV projects and commercials are sometimes thought of as trivial, but they have a serious influence on culture standards. They sell us values, images, concepts of success and worth and tell us who we are and who we should be in addition to selling us millions of products that we may or may not need.

Because my clients are responsible for spending anywhere from $20,000 on up to millions of dollars of clients' money, there is *a lot* of pressure to please their client. They take it very seriously and have zero tolerance for actors that do not. They spend a lot of time trying to get the job and then the rest of the time trying to keep their client happy!

COMMERCIALS

Commercials are the "bread and butter" of smaller markets. They can be *very* lucrative for actors, especially if they pay residuals. Residuals are ongoing payments to the actor for each repeat cycle that the commercial is aired. Actors can make upwards of $250 to $5,000 in one day shooting a commercial. This will significantly increase with each airing as well if the commercial goes national. I have seen actors make over $20,000 just on one commercial shoot.

THE CREATIVE PROCESS

In a nutshell, the industry client has a film, TV project or commercial to be made.
The "creatives" (script writers, directors, producers, artists, etc.) work very hard at bringing ideas, whether their own or their clients, to the pre-production process. This is the process that is involved with the prep work needed prior to the actual filming. I am normally contacted for my services during this pre-production process.

KEY PLAYERS IN THE INDUSTRY

The Client: *This is the person, business, studio, or corporation (entity) that I like to refer to as "the man behind the scenes", like in the Wizard of Oz. They pay the bill and they are the boss.*

Producer: *The producer oversees the job and assembles the production staff. They also control the entire budget for the project and are responsible for the hiring of a casting director. I also refer to the producer or production company or ad agency that hires me as the "client" in this book.*

Director*: The director is the driving creative force, who directs the spot and is heavily involved in the casting process. Directors are either employed by a production company, or studio or they work independently.*

Crew*: The crew is the rest of the key players that include the director of photography, script writers, grips (people who do the technical setup), hair/makeup artists, production assistants and casting director.*

SUMMARY: A BILLION-DOLLAR INDUSTRY

1. Technology has completely transformed how the industry sells their products.
2. A casting director is hired due to his/her ability to put together auditions and tap into local talent resources.
3. Films, TV shows and commercials have a serious influence on culture standards.
4. Industry clients work hard to get the job and harder to keep their client happy.
5. Commercials are the bread and butter of smaller markets.
6. Understand who the key players are in the industry.

CHAPTER 2

THE ACTING BIZ

Being an actor takes a lot of patience, perseverance, luck and timing. We are *all* born with innate talents (talents you are born with), but it is such a small part of being successful in the industry. Clients may not choose the most talented actor of the bunch but choose the one they feel has the look they want and will be the easiest to work with. I have seen this happen again and again. There are so many talented people, but the clients choose talent they feel comfortable, are directable and will do a good performance on camera. There are so many variables that come into play but if the actors make the client feel uncomfortable for whatever reason, they will not get hired.

AGENTS

A lot of people starting out in the industry usually think they must get an agent. They are not sure what an agent does, but they feel they need one right off the bat. Agents are a licensed entity that sign the actor to a contract with specific terms in place. The agents try to secure auditions for their actors and handle communication between their actors and casting directors and clients. The agent makes money off the actor when they book a job in the form of a commission which can be anywhere from 10% to 50% of the actor's earnings. The problem is an agent normally requires that you have a good amount of on camera experience, current professional headshots and maybe even an acting reel before signing you. Agents may charge a small yearly web/admin fee as well to their actors.

Casting Companies

I have seen the industry change tremendously over the past twenty-two years regarding how actors are found and discovered. The internet and the need for diverse and new talent have dictated these changes. Actors are now able to promote themselves online and connect with industry clients through local and national websites on a regular basis. There are a few casting companies that have their own databases such as my company, MovieWork Now LLC. I coordinate and hold auditions and handle the communication between talent and clients without taking a commission from talent earnings. I also assist clients that like to do their casting in-house but need submissions from actors and do not know where to go. I can post their casting needs on my site and then also send it out to our actors listed in our database. The actors can immediately apply to the project and their submission gets to our client very quickly. Production companies love this because it saves them time and money.

At MovieWorkNow.com actors can create their online profile and receive casting alerts. For a small subscription fee, they can receive priority in casting and additional online tools. Check us out at www.movieworknow.com.

MAKING A LIVING AS AN ACTOR

While working in the industry can be very lucrative, most actors I know make an actual living doing something else. I meet teachers, waiters, lawyers, financial consultants, salespeople, pilots, blue collar types, athletes, stay at home moms and personal trainers at my auditions. Bottom line is don't depend on this type of work to pay the bills. A word of caution regarding payment as I have seen this again and again with new talent; if you land a booking please do not fantasize about receiving or spending those earnings next week. Also try not to act like my Grandma Genia who would walk by her mail box daily to see if her social security check has come in the mail. Payment does take a while to receive. The ad agency gets paid first then it trickles down from there. Get used to this! If you landed a cool job it is worth the wait! Many of our actors who have done their homework are receiving checks monthly!

GET TO KNOW YOUR PRODUCT OR BRAND

Here is the big secret and what it is all boiled down to! The key ingredient is that *you* are the actual product or brand! Simply stated *you* are selling yourself. You must define your personality not by what you want to be but by what you are. So many times, actors will try to audition for roles they do not fit, or their agent will submit them for roles they do not match.

What are you selling? Analyze where you fit in and sell yourself accordingly. Keep in mind, no actor is right for every part, they all find their niche and so can you!

SMALLER MARKETS

When casting in a smaller market, many times dual casting auditions will be held in a bigger city, like Los Angeles, Miami, Chicago or New York. Flying in another actor, who did a better job than a local actor, appears to be no problem for bigger budget films and commercials. Smaller market actors have some very stiff competition, so keep reading!

I have also witnessed the opposite many times, though. For instance, an international ad agency came to me for casting, hesitant about the Arizona talent pool and wondering whether we'd find decent actors. They were used to the larger cities, so were more than a little worried. After the casting, they were really impressed with what our state had to offer. They exclusively booked our actors for their shoot and did not hire actors from out of state. I have the hard-working acting pool to thank for taking it seriously and helping to make our jobs successful.

The good news is with the today's available technology you do not have to live in a larger city, like New York or LA to get work in the industry. Productions film everywhere including smaller markets which can save them money. With the ability to watch audition clips online as well as utilizing Skype (yes believe it or not Skype is used for other purposes than catching up with family or video sex chatting with your boyfriend) clients can preview audition clips from the local talent prior to the shoot. Many clients do not even step foot into the state until just a few days to a week prior to the shoot. They arrive (usually stressed out, demanding and disgruntled) just in time to be involved in the call back auditions as well as to finish scouting their locations and to prep their upcoming production taking place in that state. They have a lot to accomplish in very little time!

ACTORS RATES AND USAGE

Films, TV programs and commercials have specific usage rights and payment is based on many factors. In films, the actors earn a variety of wages depending on how they are used and what roles or credits they get. The budget and the union affiliation also determine what the actor earns. Many times, they earn a day rate, weekly rate or a contracted lump sum.

Commercial pay also depends on how long the commercial will run, in how many markets it will air and what medium: TV, cable, print, new media, etc. This, in addition to the actor's role, will determine how much the actor will earn. For instance, if the run is for one year, the client and agent or actor can negotiate new rates after the year is up (if they continue to rerun the commercial). Rates are different for SAG talent (Screen Actors Guild) and non-union talent. A SAG commercial has very strict guidelines and specific rates. SAG principal actors are paid residuals if the commercial is re-aired, according to the SAG pay rates scale. SAG background extras may also earn residuals if the client did not pay for unlimited usage at the first airing. Although non-union commercials can dictate any pay rate they want I try to limit the usage to one year and keep the rates close to the SAG pay scale. It is more equitable for the actor to be paid for each airing. As a casting director, I help negotiate the best rates for the actors.

SUMMARY: THE ACTING BIZ

1. Most agents will not sign you if you are new to the industry.
2. Having online exposure is important so be sure to create your profile at www.movieworknow.com
3. Clients may not choose the most talented actor but instead choose the easiest one to work with.
4. Do not depend on this type of work to pay the bills.
5. Learn your product...which is *you!*
6. You are selling your personality.
7. Today's technology allows clients to preview talent prior to coming to town.
8. Rates depend on the usage, role, union affiliation, and the budget of the client.

CHAPTER 3

UNIONS AND THEIR JURISDICTIONS

There are three unions that represent the industry: SAG, AFTRA and AEA. Each one governs specific areas of the business. As of March 30, 2012, SAG and AFTRA have merged which increases their bargaining power. Be sure to learn more at the websites listed below.

1. *Screen Actors Guild* (SAG) has jurisdiction over actors appearing in film, television commercial, new media (internet, mobile devices), industrials, as well as voice-overs. http://www.sagaftra.org/

2. *The American Federation of Television and Radio Artists* (AFTRA) has jurisdiction over live and taped television shows and commercials, soap operas, disc jockeys and radio performers. http://www.sagaftra.org/

3. *Actors Equity Association* (AEA) has jurisdiction over performers and managers in live theatre. http://www.actorsequity.org/

BECOMING A MEMBER

If the market is smaller, non-union projects may be more of the norm and many actors will delay joining a union until they have gained experience, and many opt not to join at all. The initiation fees may be in the thousands and there are yearly dues required.

Once an actor joins a union, he is unable to work on non-union projects (governed by that union). If talent moving to a larger market, where most of the work is union, I recommend joining, as soon as possible.

Benefits of joining a union include: support with contract negotiations, provision of pension and health benefits, industry tools, publications and other resources.

HOW TO JOIN A UNION

SAG: these are the most common ways to join SAG.

- You are booked as a principal performer or in a speaking role for a SAG film, television commercial, program or video project.
- You are booked as a SAG background actor on three SAG projects.
- You have been a member of an affiliate union (like AFTRA and AEA) for one year and have worked at least once in that union's jurisdiction.

AFTRA: the easiest union to join (due to the merger the rules may have changed).

- Fill out an application and pay the membership fees.

AEA: three methods to join.

- You have been employed under an Equity contract.
- You have been a member of an affiliate union (like SAG or AFTRA).
- You get a job with a theatre, as a production person or understudy, and carn your way through the Equity Membership Candidate Program.

RIGHT-TO-WORK STATES

In a right-to-work state, a company cannot exclude you from employment because of non-membership in an acting union. Currently there are twenty-five right-to-work states in the United States. For more information and to see if your state is listed go to http://www.ncsl.org/research/labor-and-employment/right-to-work-laws-and-bills.aspx.

To be clear though: even in a right to work state, a union member cannot work on non-union jobs. It is always necessary to follow the rules of union membership and not violate any signed agreement.

SUMMARY: UNIONS AND THEIR JURISDICTIONS

1. The three most popular acting unions are SAG, AFTRA and AEA.
2. Depending upon the market, actors will need to determine if joining a union is the right thing to do.
3. A union can offer benefits to the actor and provide guidance with contracts, rates, and industry-related issues.
4. A right to work state will attract non-union work, so union actors will miss out on those opportunities.

CHAPTER 4

TRAINING

Although this book is geared towards the actual audition process, this is not a guarantee that you will do well in front of the camera. Just showing up and saying the lines perfectly while having the deer in the headlights look once the casting director says "action" is not attractive to our clients. The audition room is not the place to learn how to act.

In my opinion, the best way to learn acting technique is to train. You do not have to spend a fortune or commit a lot of time to classes either. There are usually inexpensive classes or weekend workshops offered in a city near you.

Many industries involve training and ours is no different. An athlete works out and constantly tries to improve his performance or game; professional sales people attend sales training seminars; realtors attend workshops on an ongoing basis, and pilots and flight attendants continue to attend training throughout their careers. Actors must also continue to train and work at bettering their performances.

Adults that want to work in the industry should take a basic acting technique class or scene study class or commercial audition class when starting out. Training is one of the best ways to transition from inexperienced actor to working actor. Training is also very therapeutic, and it allows you to see other actors making mistakes and blowing lines.

Children can get by on their natural personality and charm until about age eight and after that they will encounter more challenging roles and more competition. Taking an acting class is a fun way for them to explore acting with their own age group. I also highly recommend for print models that want to cross over into the acting realm, that they take acting classes to extend their number of years in the industry. They will quickly learn that they cannot get by on their looks alone and the savvy print model will take the steps necessary to train and improve their hire-ability. They will want to begin training early on, so that, when they are older, and the print modeling jobs are fewer, they can still be involved in the lucrative field of film, TV and/or commercials.

TYPES OF TRAINING

Who can you trust to teach acting? Local acting schools conduct ongoing training classes in scene study and various acting techniques (Meisner, Stanislavski's system, classical acting, method acting, practical aesthetics) as well as improvisation, commercials acting, cold reading, teleprompter and monologues; private coaches offer various training techniques; casting directors or "travelling" casting directors may offer an audition or acting workshop; Large and small theatre companies offer classes; local universities or community colleges offer acting classes as well as various film production classes; and last on my totem pole are the modeling/acting franchises. There is not one right way to train: take what you can from your training and then use your own personality to do the rest.

ACTING SCHOOLS

Some of the acting schools with which I am familiar offer a variety of classes, which are taught by local, professional working actors, who have the experience and knowledge to educate you. They know what it is like to start out in the industry and they have worked at their craft over many years. Often, after your completion of a round of classes, a local showcase, put together by the school, will allow you to show your skills to *local* talent agents and casting directors, and sometimes even directors and producers. You may even get picked up by an agent!

If you want to do commercials, I recommend that you take a commercial acting class. Check to see that their coaches have credits to their name or booked jobs themselves. Also make sure the class uses a video recorder to record your performance and that you get plenty of time in front of the camera.

I have attended several local showcases and have found some outstanding actors. After a showcase, I called on one of the actors to assist me with upcoming auditions for a feature film. His duty was to read the lines with the other actors during the auditions. The director was so impressed with him that he gave him a big part and hired him to work as his assistant during the entire shoot! The experience he received was invaluable and the contacts he made, priceless: all from taking some classes with a local acting facility. He now lives in Los Angeles, continues to train, and is a very busy, working actor.

PRIVATE ACTING COACHES

Taking lessons with a private acting coach can be a good way to get some one-on-one training. Please make sure the trainer is or was a working actor and booked jobs continually. Trust your judgment; you must feel comfortable with meeting the trainer one on one. It is never a good idea to leave a minor alone, in this situation.

CASTING DIRECTOR WORKSHOPS

Participation in workshops given by casting directors can be an effective way to learn *basic* audition skills. To get to know different styles of auditioning, by all means take their class; otherwise, look elsewhere to learn acting technique unless they were a successful former actor.

"TRAVELLING" CASTING DIRECTOR WORKSHOPS

There are casting directors that travel to different cities and hold workshops for the local actors and this is a big business and creates good income supplementation for them. Most of them are based in Los Angeles. Keep in mind they most likely are not holding an actual audition but are only giving classes on how to audition or other acting techniques. They may make you feel like you will get a part in a big production taking place in which ever big city they are based in. The actual chance of those casting directors using you for a future project is very slim to none. Most production companies will not do a long-distance hire, meaning they will not hire you if you do not live in the state where the shoot is taking place.

I recommend you enroll in *local* acting classes and be seen by *local* casting directors.

ACTING/MODELING FRANCHISES

Acting franchises maintain nation-wide offices and offer modeling and acting classes. However, their prices are high, and the acting coaches may not be the most qualified. You may be invited to join an upcoming travelling convention (like IMTA or International Model & Talent Association) that takes place in New York or Los Angeles, for a chance to audition and train with big-name casting directors or talent agents. These conventions cost $5000 to $10,000 or more! While there are success stories of talent that has been discovered at these conventions, do your research and feel comfortable with the money obligation for your *chance* of discovery through an acting/modeling franchise or convention.

A word of caution, there are also companies that go from town to town and parade as "talent scouts" and hold an "audition" in a local hotel. They schedule you to come in and put you through their "screening" process and then tell you that only a few will be chosen. They then call EVERYONE that attended the "audition" and ask them for large sums of money for guess what…acting classes!

THEATRE

The local theatre is the ideal place to get training on how to be a theatre actor and perform in front of a live audience. I encourage children to start out at the local youth theatres. Some hold classes year-round and even offer theatre camps during the summer and school breaks. Participation in these events allows kids to gain the confidence to do very well at commercial, film and TV auditions. The same goes for adults: you do not have to be young to reap the rewards of this type of training.

Theatre actors are some of the best talent in town!

CHECKING CREDITS

Here is a tip regarding actor's credits. You can go to a website titled the Internet Movie Database at http://www.imdb.com/ and type in your acting coach's name to see if they have any credits listed from their days in front of the camera. This is a great place to see their experience and most actors are very proud to have their credits listed. IMDB does not list all commercial projects but it is a great way for actors, directors, producers, crew people and even casting directors to promote their work.

SUMMARY: TRAINING

1. Very few people have the natural ability to handle auditions.
2. Training is the best way to learn audition skills and acting technique.
3. Local acting companies may offer a variety of acting classes.
4. Private acting instructors can give you undivided attention.
5. Be sure to take *commercial* acting classes to better prepare you for commercial auditions.
6. Casting director workshops can help you to learn basic audition skills.
7. Rather than enrolling in "traveling" casting director workshops, invest in classes with local acting coaches.
8. Theatre companies and community colleges are both great places to train.
9. Franchises/conventions may not have the best acting coaches and can be pricey.
10. Make sure acting classes are taught by former (or current) working actors.

CHAPTER 5

WHERE DO YOU FIT IN?

Unfortunately, people want to submit themselves to jobs they do not fit. They have not come to terms or figured out where they fit in. Knowing your marketability and what you have to offer is crucial to working in this industry. Once again, *you* are the product so get to know your product! *Be realistic* about what type you are commercially. What is your age range, physical look and personality?

When you watch commercials, study the actors to see their looks, character, and charisma. Get an idea as to where you would fit in. Are you a *professional (doctor, lawyer), geek/nerd, playmate, athlete, military, hippie, mom/dad type, CEO, blue-collar type, sexy heroine or hero, ditzy blonde, athlete, granny, grandpa, fast food counter guy, spokesperson, swimsuit model, office worker?* There are so many possibilities and you may fall into several categories but there will be many you do not fit. So, find your niche and pursue these types of roles.

Here are some "looks" that are common in the industry.

Character: likeable, real-person type, may have a few extra pounds, pronounced facial features or even downright funny looking.

Street Funny: terrific sense of humor derived from "living it real" on the street and hanging out with be boppers and local boys, makes funny comments about real life, most importantly uses local slang words (depending on where they live) when expressing their humor (examples: "just sayin", "that's how you dooze it", "fer real?", "lets bounce", "tru dat" "no need", "baby mama" or "baby daddy".

Edgy: hip, funky hair, tattoos, body piercings, may work at coffee houses.

Average American (what commercials want): generic middle-American look, well proportioned, semi-attractive, healthy-looking, happy.

Pretty or Handsome: natural and approachable; not a fashion model or too glamorous.

Model Types: above average to extremely good looking; usually have high cheekbones, perfect teeth, excellent skin and a well-proportioned, toned body. *(This is a category that many people try to fit in (remember those mirrors with rose colored glasses?) but in reality, only a small percentage of people are truly model material.)*

Quirky or Off-beat: different from the average middle-American (maybe very pretty, but with a big nose).

Urban/city Type: yuppie, with a stylish edge or a hip and trendy look. These days may be sporting a long beard or what I call a lumberjack beard. Not sure why this is so popular, but I see these bearded faces everywhere now!

Suburban Type: casual, relaxed, sporty, rugged, outdoorsy type.

Bad Guy/Thug: shady looking, may be big in physique, causes people to cross the street to avoid them, shifty eyes (okay that was more of the silent movie era and they are subtler these days).

Ambiguous Ethnicity: mixed-race look or indeterminate background; mulatto or slightly Latin look. As my daughter says, "everybody is having sex with everyone so of course we are all blended". This is very popular request in commercial advertising.

YOUR "LOOK"

Be realistic about your physical appearance. Rather than focus on what you would like to be, take a good look at yourself in the mirror and realize your true attributes, with a realistic approach. Ask friends or family members what they think your type is (make sure they like you first!): you may be surprised by what you hear.

Keep in mind with film and commercials the creators love to use "real" and "approachable" types. You do not have to be perfect to get work; just be realistic about what you have to offer. Rest assured: there are always roles available for *all* looks and levels of attractiveness.

BODY TYPE

Most of us are not Victoria's Secret models and life would be very boring if that were the case (although the men reading this will think otherwise). As hard as it is to accept, it is okay if you have a few extra pounds on you, wrinkles on your face or ears you can tie in a knot. When an audition calls for a slim build, then that is exactly what is needed. If the client requests a plump businessman or gray-haired granny, then that is what I will offer.

Also, casting swimsuit models requires very physically fit talent who are not shy about being partially clothed. If you are shy or uncomfortable parading in a swimsuit, it is best to pass on this type of audition. Never try out for a role when you are not comfortable with the requirements. I have witnessed this during several Go Daddy auditions. As you all may know Go Daddy does very titillating commercials and requests "hot chicks" in skimpy clothes. During several swimsuit auditions I always encounter the model that absolutely hates showing her body even though she is a "model" ...hello!

YOUR SKILLS

Do not try to pass yourself off as an expert unless you can prove your abilities (examples are: languages, experience with teleprompters, knowledge of a certain topic, and accents). I have done several bilingual castings of Spanish speakers and the clients always want *fluent* speakers. Time and again, actors claim to be fluent and, when they show up, can barely get by. It never works out, so please, be realistic about your skills.

Same for "athlete" castings, a handful of actors usually embellish their ability in the given sport (i.e. golf, football or baseball). The clients can always spot the amateur making it quite embarrassing for the actor. If you do not have experience in the given sport or your skill level is not up to par with the casting request, please pass on the opportunity.

I also had an actor get booked for a commercial where a teleprompter was being used and he was not trained on this. The client was so upset and used me as a sounding board to vent his frustration at this actor's inability to use a teleprompter.

DIALECTS/ACCENTS

Unless you can master a believable accent, use only your real native accent during auditions. I had an audition where a British accent was needed so I brought in several males who claimed to do a British accent and a couple of native British-accented males. The males who were not native always fell back into their American accent during their read; they were focusing on their lines and the accent went by the wayside. Exceptions to this are Christian Bale...*hubba hubba*! Also, never add an accent unless it is requested. For some reason, actors tend to add a Southern dialect to their auditions, without being asked to do so.

During bilingual Spanish castings, commercial clients will usually request *non-accented* Spanish speakers. I had no idea what the heck that meant until a client made fun of my "accented" Spanish I used while reading with the actors during their audition. I finally figured out they do not want the dialogue to represent a certain region or country.

YOUR AGE

Although growing older is never fun, actors need to be realistic about how old they look. Older actors frequently want to try out for much younger roles. They all say the same thing: "I don't look my age". If I had a dollar every time I have heard this over the years I would be very rich! I hear this from both men and women. Unfortunately, nine times out of ten, they *do* look their age. The best rule of thumb is: do not exceed a five-year difference from your age. For instance, if you are 50, your age range would be 45 to 55 years old. Also, if you are a minor, do not apply for adult roles, as there may be legal reasons why you cannot be hired, for instance a casino or lottery commercial.

Agents are notorious for submitting talent that do not fit as they want as many of their people as possible to have opportunities to audition.

SUMMARY: WHERE DO YOU FIT IN?

1. Objectively assess your age range, look and personality.
2. Be realistic about what you have to offer: are you a leading-lady, girl next door or executive?
3. Real and approachable types are very popular and there are opportunities for everyone.
4. Rather than what you want to be, focus on what you really are.
5. Do not audition for swimsuit jobs if it makes you uncomfortable.
6. Never exaggerate your skills and abilities.
7. Do not claim language fluency you do not have.
8. Never add an accent unless it is requested.
9. When responding to a casting call, which specifies age, stay within a five-year limit, either way, from your actual age.
10. Minors are *not* normally considered for over age eighteen roles.

CHAPTER 6

TYPES OF WORK AVAILABLE

There are so many different projects and creative things an actor can work on to gain experience. From block buster feature films to live promotional events a new actor can determine how they fit in the industry and what they get a calling for. It is important to follow your heart as an actor and focus on things that make you feel good and are fun to work on. Although it is very long hours and very tiring to be on set all day there should be some enjoyment for you as an actor or you will quickly burn out.

The industry can be full of cynical and jaded industry types and may consider you just a moveable prop. I have also been a part of the most amazing crews and magic truly can happen on set when there is certain camaraderie among the crew.

STUDIO FEATURE FILMS

A studio feature film, also known as movie studio film is backed by a major entertainment company or motion picture company. They are privately owned and have their own studio facilities. They tend to shoot what they think the average American wants to see and many times they use the same formula or recipe because unfortunately the average American is the "average" American.

INDEPENDENT FEATURE FILMS

An independent film is a feature film that is produced mostly or completely outside of the major film studio system. They are produced and distributed by independent companies and can also have major marketing campaigns and worldwide releases like studio films. Independent films are recognized by the filmmaker's stylish personal artistic vision and edgy scripts and topics. They usually have unique perspectives and a non-cookie cutter view of the world. They are many times even better than a studio film if the funding is in place and many get by on a shoestring budget.

SHORT FILMS

A short film is a feature film wrapped in shrink wrap and shrunk down to fit about 40 minutes of screen time including the credits. Many times, a short film is produced to market an upcoming feature film that the production company is going to shoot. Many new filmmakers make shorts as well to get their foot in the door and gain experience. Working in short films is a great way for actors starting out to get meatier roles and exposure.

INDUSTRIAL FILMS

Companies utilize industrial films for marketing or training purposes within their own industry or trade. These are very similar to "educational" films. The video content varies depending on the needs of the clients or companics. Many times, they request spokesperson types and on- camera announcer type of talent (I call them robots). Luckily clients today are requesting more "real people" types to portray their characters.

THEATRE PLAYS

A play is the written works of playwrights and the actors perform live in front of an audience or better known as a doing a live theatrical performance. One must be a very strong actor to perform live in front of hundreds of people. Plays can be performed On- Broadway, Off- Broadway, in regional and community theatres as well as college or school productions. Once again some of my best actors are theatre actors!

TELEVISION PROJECTS

Television projects are constantly being filmed throughout the globe. From TV movies, mini-series, episodic series, documentaries, *to* talk shows, reality shows and of course commercials. Most people watch

TV to see their favorite show or to simply "zone out" after a hard day at work, working for "the man". I do enjoy a good movie or documentary but in the rare instances that I actually watch television, it is usually for the commercials. The Super Bowl is a favorite time to watch very big budget commercials and you can learn so much from studying them, so make this a part of your training. Go to YouTube http://www.youtube.com to see hundreds of them. If you know the director's name for your upcoming audition, you may be able to find some of his actual work on YouTube, as well. You can also do this for film and television directors.

PROMOTIONS

Promotions are live events where companies rent space and have a presence at the venue. They like to hire outgoing promotional models to assist them with handing out flyers, educating event goers or demonstrating the latest gadget the consumer just can't live without. "Promotional Model" does not always mean you have to be beautiful or handsome. A lot of companies like to have "real people" or average types as well. Many clients pay from $12.00 to $25.00 per hour for the model's time which adds up when putting in a full day.

PRINT WORK

Print modeling is a huge industry and consists of editorial, fashion, catalogue, swimwear, lingerie, nude, and advertising print. You may feel you have to be tall and gorgeous to do print work like the high fashion industry but many of my print clients request all types of people. Talent can earn thousands of dollars for one day of work doing print work.

WORLD WIDE WEB

The latest and greatest at least in my life time is the invention of the world wide web. I do remember when we built our first website back in the late 90's! A lot of you literally grow up with a computer in you these days so this is nothing new, but *we* consider this a virtual vending machine due to the enormous content that can be created, watched and bought. Advertisers (and Actors!) can promote their products, films, commercials and businesses 24/7 online and new faces are in high demand for online content.

SUMMARY: TYPES OF WORK AVAILABLE

1. There are so many creative projects for actors to work on.
2. The industry has many cynical types but also amazing camaraderie among crew members.
3. Studio films are backed by major motion picture companies and tend to have a cookie cutter view of the world.
4. Independent filmmakers are more visionary and tend to think outside of the box.
5. Corporations and businesses use industrial films to educate their employees or peers.
6. Some of my best actors are theatre actors!
7. Television can also offer more things for you besides allowing you to "zone out", it can also be educational such as when studying commercials and actor's expressions and reactions etc.
8. Companies and corporations like to hire outgoing promotional models to assist them with handing out flyers, educating event goers or demonstrating the latest gadget.
9. Print work is a huge industry and there is a need for all types.

CHAPTER 7

TYPES OF AUDITIONS

There are several types of auditions you may encounter and the more you practice with each type, the easier it gets. The following are examples of the different types of auditions. In an upcoming chapter titled: *Preparing for Your Performance* I give you directions, advice and examples in more detail.

SCRIPT OR SIDES

In this most common type of audition, you are given a side, which is a portion of the script that has your character's lines. It may be one page or multiple pages, from the script. Many times, the director selects the sides, depending upon what he or she wants to see at the audition. You may be given this in advance or at the audition when you arrive. At most of my auditions, the actor has received the script or side a day or two in advance.

STORYBOARD

A storyboard is an illustration of the script that shows the action along with the lines (if there are any) and stage direction, in cartoon like format. They are very common in commercial auditions, as they help in visualizing the action, expressions, reactions, etc. Some auditions offer only a storyboard to study; others provide the side along with the storyboard, in advance.

COLD READ

In a cold read, you are given the side, script or storyboard at the actual audition, with very little time to prepare in advance. You are usually allowed to hold the side during the audition for reference (more about cold reads in the chapter *Memorizing your lines)*.

MONOLOGUE

A monologue is a one- or two-minute paragraph, which you have memorized. It is a scene with you as the only actor. Usually, you will be told what type of monologue to prepare: comedic or dramatic. Monologues are very popular in theatre auditions and seldom used at a commercial casting.

IMPROVISATIONAL AUDITION

Improvisation is acting without a script. Although there is nothing to prepare, classes in improv technique are helpful. The goal is to remain calm and open to ideas that will be thrown at you at the audition.

INTERVIEW AUDITION

An interview audition is very common when casting print talent or children. Along with having the required "look," you will be presenting a preview of your personality (will you be positive and easy to work with?). Although these can be fun, they are also very nerve-wracking if you are not comfortable talking about yourself.

SUMMARY: TYPES OF AUDITIONS

1. Take classes that are specific to the different types of auditions.
2. Auditions normally have a script available a day or two in advance.
3. A storyboard helps you see the action, reactions, and expressions of the characters.
4. A cold read is a script or side given to you when you arrive to the audition.
5. Monologue pieces should be well rehearsed and ready to perform.
6. Improvisational auditions are off-the-cuff. Keep an open mind and be ready to accept the information and direction given to you.
7. Interview auditions allow the clients to get a feel for your personality.

CHAPTER 8

YOUR AUDITION NOTIFICATION

Okay, so you have been asked to come in and audition for a project. You obviously are being requested due to your look or skills fitting a given role. You are probably thinking "oh my god I got called for an audition, what do I do?" Self-doubt may start to settle in because you do not know what to expect. It is normal to be nervous and just knowing what to expect is half the battle.

THE BUSINESS OF ACTING

A cliché, but true: *acting is a business*. The more you take care of your business, the more opportunities you will have. Treat the audition like a small homework assignment. How you prepare for your audition and behave during the audition process will greatly affect your chances of success. Mistakes are not always the fault of new actors either; they happen to all levels of talent.

Industry people are notoriously cynical. Despite their responsibility of pleasing their clients, they are often the first ones in the line of fire when things go wrong. They place a great deal of trust on the actor when thousands of dollars are at stake, so, they prefer doing business with actors they like and can trust. Remember, you are selling yourself always, so, you will need to prove that you are easy to work with and can handle whatever is asked of you.

PREPARATION/CHECKLIST

Too many times the actor does not have all the necessary information prior to the audition. I can't stress this next point enough: it is *the actor's responsibility* to have all the information necessary to ensure a great audition!

Here is a basic checklist of questions to ask the casting director or your agent before each audition:

1. Where is the audition?
2. What time is my appointment?
3. What is the project?
4. What is my role?
5. What is the rate?
6. What is the usage?
7. Is there a script?
8. How and when will I receive the script?
9. What is the proper way to dress?
10. What must I bring?
11. When is the callback date?

12. When is the shoot date?
13. Do you have any other details about my character?
14. Who is the director? (we may not even know yet, but you can ask)

YOUR AVAILABILITY

Check your schedule before committing to your audition appointment and do not audition if you are unavailable for the shoot dates. At a recent audition for a casino commercial, an actor announced he was not available for the shoot dates, but still wanted to be put on camera. Perhaps, he thought everyone would fall in love with him and rearrange the shoot to accommodate him. Suffice it to say, I did not put him on camera and I had to inform his agent that he wasted everyone's time by showing up. Of course, he told his agent he *was* available, so this was news to them too and they were not happy the actor made them look bad.

Please do your best to also be available for the callback date. Rarely does an actor get chosen who did not come to callback. Even though they may have done a fantastic job at the first audition, clients are way too cautious about choosing an actor they could not personally meet first.

Do not have any conflicts at all during the shoot date(s). Consider most shoot days to be all-day events. It is highly unprofessional, if you are booked for a job, and must leave to pick up your kids. Do not commit to the audition until you have checked your availability and conflicts.

UNDERSTAND YOUR ROLE AND GET YOUR SCRIPT

Actors frequently attend the audition, only to say they "did not get a script" or they "do not know which role to read," and usually blame their agents. Once again, *it is always the responsibility of the actor* to understand what the audition is for, what the role is and whether there is a script. E-mail is not perfect; maybe the agent or casting assistant did send it, but it went to the junk folder or a different e-mail address. Once you realize you did not receive it, as promised, call them to tell them to resend it! You may have been selected for two different roles, so, be prepared and make sure you received both scripts.

WARDROBE

Prepare what you will wear to the audition, in advance. Bad wardrobe choices do not permit us to see the actor's audition session because they are so distracting. Believe me; I have seen some crazy ensembles over the past twenty years! From busy shirts with crazy patterns to pants so tight I could see their nether regions! Keep your wardrobe simple. Wear comfortable clothes that allow you to move and do not distract.

Basic guidelines for any type of on-camera work:

1. Avoid wearing white: the camera typically finds the brightest object in the picture, which can make the other colors too dark.
2. Avoid wearing black: black needs more lighting and that causes everything else in the picture to wash out.
3. Avoid highly saturated colors, like red, which can bleed into other parts of the picture.
4. Avoid wearing pin stripes, checks, herringbone patterns and small intricate designs: they appear to vibrate on camera and can cause what is known as a *"moiré."*
5. Avoid message t-shirts: too distracting.
6. Avoid flashy, dangly, or noisy jewelry.
7. Avoid outdated outfits (trashy 70's or 80's stuff), unless the role calls for them.
8. Ladies avoid revealing clothes, short skirts, bare midriffs, low necklines or too tight clothing. We want to focus on your face, not your body parts or lack of clothes.
9. *DO* incorporate blue into your wardrobe, as blue represents positive energy and can make you feel calm and relaxed.

10.   In addition to blue; browns, tans, greens and purple are all good colors, if they are not too bright. Pastels, solid colors and clothes you feel comfortable in and can move well in are best.

Actors often ask whether to dress the part. Sometimes, the answer is most definitely yes (like when we are casting swimsuit models). Otherwise, simply dress to *imply* the character. Do not go overboard.

Specific audition clothes that you can pull out in a pinch will come in very handy, especially if you have figured out your "brand" or "look." Have choices available: do you have a suit for the CEO type? do you have sporty clothes? frazzled mom clothes? blue-collar clothes? etc. Go to the thrift store and pick up wardrobe options for very little money, especially things you normally may not wear like a business suit.

MAKE-UP

Make-up makes a difference and is important. At the minimum, powder your nose, forehead and face to eliminate shiny spots. Men powder your forehead and bald spots. Females wear a natural foundation, under eye cover, powder, mascara, blush and light lipstick. Do not wear too shiny lip-gloss or foundation that does not match your skin tone, as this is very noticeable on camera. Regarding minors, we prefer they remain natural, so a little powder will do.

HAIR

Have an updated style and natural color that compliments your skin tone. Avoid strange colors, unless the role calls for them. Hair must not hang in your face during the audition. During a sport commercial audition, I held, one of the females had longer hair and a piece of her hair was covering her left eye but even more hilarious was it went in and out of her mouth the entire time she was auditioning. I was sure she was going to correct this, but she kept on talking with her hair in her mouth! I had no idea how her performance was because all I could do was focus on her hair going in and out of her mouth. I asked her to tuck it behind her ear and made her do the audition again.

It is best to bring something to tie your hair up with just in case. I have had many directors ask the females to put their hair up in a ponytail away from their face during a callback audition.

Regarding wigs: I do not encourage the wearing of a wig to your audition. Clients notice the wig and the talent rarely gets chosen, if at all. There are instances where the client will want to provide a wig for the actual shoot; let them determine whether this is necessary.

TATTOOS/BODY PIERCINGS

The industry does request talent with large visible tattoos and body piercings at times. Especially when looking for edgy types. It can also hinder you from getting jobs if this was not requested. If you have visible tattoos and it is not in the role description, then please inform the casting director so there are not any surprises on set for the director and make-up artist. If you have facial piercings, other than earrings, do not wear your jewelry during the audition. Why give the client reasons to not select you or not even watch your audition? You may be a brilliant actor, so, why hurt your chances.

Summary: Your Audition

NOTIFICATION

1. It is normal to be nervous when you are called in for an audition.
2. Acting is a business and clients hire actors they like and can trust.
3. Prepare a checklist of questions to ask your casting director or agent before your audition.
4. Check your schedule before committing to an audition appointment.
5. It is your responsibility to make sure you get a script and to know which your role is.
6. Prepare your audition wardrobe well in advance and keep your clothes simple.
7. Collect clothes specifically for your "brand" or "look."
8. Wear some powder to eliminate shiny spots; keep makeup simple.
9. Wear a hair color that compliments your skin tone (avoid strange colors unless the audition calls for them).
10. Keep hair out of the face and away from the eyes.
11. Bring something to tie your hair up with.
12. Avoid wearing wigs.
13. Take out your piercings and inform them of your visible tattoos (if not requested) for the audition.

CHAPTER 9

GETTING AROUND THE SCRIPT

When you receive a script, most of the information is there, right in front of you. You need to learn how to break it down and know which lines to memorize. Sprinkled in the script are camera instructions, which let us know the point of view of the camera. Also included is stage direction, which tells the actor a variety of things (his reactions, whether implied or obvious, who he is talking to, and much more).

STAGE DIRECTION

The stage direction is sometimes noted in parentheses, is italicized or is in all capitals, and it always stands out from the actual lines. Many times, the actors miss these important clues, making it easy to misunderstand the direction of the speaking lines.

NARRATOR

Lines for the Narrator or Voice-over are lines you *never* say unless trying out for those roles.

SCRIPT REVISION

Another very important thing is the date the script was approved is usually located at the top of the page. There may even be a revision number after this date that lets you know which revision you have. This is important: if you are invited to a callback, you must make sure you have the most current script, as there may have been changes from the version you received at the initial casting session.

COMMON DIRECTIONS

VO or ANNCR VO:	Announcer or voice over
OC:	Off camera
SFX-FX:	Special effects or sound effects
(like music)	
EXT and INT:	Exterior or interior shots
MUSIC:	Music starts or fades
POV:	Point of view

SUMMARY: GETTING AROUND THE SCRIPT

1. Look for the clues, stage direction, and camera direction which are in most scripts.
2. Never read the lines of narrator or voice over, unless you are auditioning for this.
3. Pay attention to the script revision date.
4. Learn the common abbreviated directions which are in most scripts.

CHAPTER 10

ANALYZING SCRIPTS

People tend to think auditioning for films and commercials is very different but to be honest they are very similar as to how you would approach your audition. Once again, I am not writing this to teach you how to act. You can take scene study classes to gain experience working with other actors and to get used to longer scripts, but the audition process is basically the same. You come in and give a believable performance and do your best no matter the length of dialogue given you for your read.

First, read the script through to the end for maximum comprehension, without acting it out loud. When you break it down, line-by-line, answer these basic questions: What are the characters trying to say? Who is my character talking to (who is the audience)? Where am I? What is the conflict or resolution (which is common in commercial auditions)? When looking at the conflict or resolution, remember that commercials are very light-hearted: most frustrations have humor in them. Remain likeable and approachable; *do not* think of yourself as selling anything! This may not be the same for a film audition though.

Begin studying the script and try to determine your beginning, end as well as your objective. Next, divide the script into moments or emotional changes. A good idea is to use a highlighter to mark your lines, so they stand out. Bring *yourself* to the character. Try to make strong choices for your emotional changes, recognizing they must also be smooth transitions. Actors that make a memorable, unique performance out of an ordinary, scripted audition will get the job.

Pick someone you know to substitute in the "who am I talking to?" question and visualize speaking to this person. Because scripts tend to be very conversational, it is important to be as real as possible and not overact the emotions. Directors do not want to see "acting" and *do* want to see "being real" or "being believable."

Practice your lines with a friend or family member, if possible. Saying them out loud is best. A word of caution: in a recent audition, the actors had to yell out the lines, as if rooting for a sports team. One of them had practiced his yelling *so* much the day before that his voice was hoarse and cracking during his audition. You *can* over rehearse your lines!

SAMPLE FEATURE FILM SIDE #1

Andy quickly breaks it, refocusing on the play.

ON STAGE

ENTER STAGE LEFT: MRS. SMITH (73), wearing an apron, a cast
iron pot in her hands. She places the pot on a small table,
then sits. She picks up a carrot from the table, peeling it.

A silence, Mr. SMITH watches her cook, his eyes hurting.

>   MR. SMITH
>   Reckon' this may be the last time I
>   see you, Little Lady.

>   MRS. SMITH
>   Don't say that, Cherokee... Don't
>   ever say that.

56   INT. COMMUNITY CENTER - NIGHT   56

A reception for the play has been set up in the lobby. Many
SENIOR COUPLES chatting, discussing. SENIORS surround Andy.
DRAMA CLUB PRESIDENT (80) talks excitedly. Andy pretends to
listen.

>   DRAMA CLUB PRESIDENT
>   We have five productions a year and
>   all the actors are from here you
>   see, but we do bring in directors
>   from elsewhere. Nothing like what
>   you do, though.

>   MARVA
>   Excuse me, Bill.

Marva pulls Andy toward Betsy, who is standing with her
grandmother drinking punch in the corner.

>   MARVA (CONT'D)
>   Betsy, this is our son Andy, from
>   Los Angeles.

Betsy smiles, playing naive. Marva puts her hand on Andy's
shoulder. Andy is embarrassed.

>   ANDY
>   Mom, we met the other day.

>   BETSY
>   It's nice to see you again, Andy.

                              MRS. SMITH
                    Go on honey...ask him.

                              MR. SMITH
                    Andy, we actually called you here
                    for something else.
                         (beat)
                    The Mrs. and I...let's see how I
                    can put this. Well, word on the
                    street is that you've got a certain
                    gift for helping people...you know,
                    with certain problems.

                              ANDY
                    I'm not sure I know what you mean?
                         (beat)
                    I'm just a Roto guy.

                              MRS. SMITH
                    But Joe and TJ said...

                              MR. SMITH
                    Honey.

                              ANDY
                    Joe and TJ said what?

                              MR. SMITH
                    Just that you had good advice.

                              ANDY
                    About what?

                              MRS. SMITH
                    You know...Sex.

Andy turns around to leave. The Smiths follow.

                              ANDY
                    I'm going to kill them.

                              MRS. SMITH
                    Please, Andy.

                              MR. SMITH
                    We're not bad people.

                              ANDY
                    You've got the wrong idea. I can't
                    help you.

Andy walks out of the door.

95   EXT. SMITH'S HOUSE - CONTINUOUS   95

        Andy exits the house, walking over toward his plumbing gear
        in the yard. Mr. Smith exits moments later.

                        MR. SMITH
                Andy, I don't have anything left in
                the tank...not anymore. I need
                guidance. And not the kind Myron
                McGill's offering, either.
                        (beat)
                Please, son...teach this old dog a
                few tricks.
                        (beat)
                No one's judging you, here.
                Just...lookin' to learn a thing or
                two, is all.

        Andy slowly turns around, staring at Mr. Smith for a long
        moment, deciding.

96   INT. SMITH'S HOUSE, LIVING ROOM - DAY   96

        Andy sits next to Mr. Smith on the couch and takes a deep
        breath.

                        ANDY
                Mr. Smith?

                        MR. SMITH
                Call me Eddie.

                        ANDY
                Okay. Eddie. I'm going to ask you
                some questions. I want you to
                really think about them...and then
                give me an answer, okay?

                        MR. SMITH
                Sure.

                        ANDY
                Do you remember the first time you
                saw your wife? The way you felt?

        Mr. Smith smiles, recalling.

                        MR. SMITH
                Oh yes. She had a smile that was
                something else. She was so
                beautiful it terrified me.
                        (MORE)

                        MR. SMITH (CONT'D)
                   But she was just the sweetest thing
                   in the world. Not a bad bone in her
                   body.

Mr. Smith glances toward the other room, then leans in to
Andy.

                        MR. SMITH (CONT'D)
                   I wanted to ravage her, you see.
                   But, back then, things moved
                   slowly. I spent many a sleepless
                   nights lying in bed, my heart
                   pounding, thinking about the moment
                   when I might get to ah... well you
                   know...

                        ANDY
                   What?

                        MR. SMITH
                   Finally get to have her.
                        (beat)
                   I feel like I can speak plainly
                   with you, Andy.

                        ANDY
                   When you finally got to have her,
                   Mr. Smith...how did that feel?

                        MR. SMITH
                   Oh Lord. I think it's the closest
                   I've ever been to heaven.

                        ANDY
                   Eddie?

                        MR. SMITH
                   Yeah?

                        ANDY
                   That little number you just told me
                   about?

                        MR. SMITH
                   Yeah?

                        ANDY
                   She's in the kitchen waiting for
                   you. And she wants you real bad.
                        (beat)
                   I want you to go in there, kiss her
                   on the back of the neck, and send
                   her over the moon.
                        (MORE)

                         ANDY (CONT'D)
                    (beat)
                 You understand?

                         MR. SMITH
                 I believe I do.

97   INT. SMITH'S HOUSE, KITCHEN - DAY   97

       Mrs. Smith spreads mayonnaise on a slice of Bread. Mr. Smith
       enters the room and comes up behind her. He grabs her arms.
       Mrs. Smith's eyes widen. Mr. Smith kisses the back of her
       neck. Mrs. Smith puts down the knife and closes her eyes.

98   INT. SMITH'S HOUSE, LIVING ROOM - DAY   98

       Andy quietly walks towards the kitchen and listens.

                         MRS. SMITH (O.S.)
                    Oh, Eddie!

       Andy's eyes widen as he exits.

       ENTER MUSIC

                                                        MONTAGE:

99   INT. TAGGERT HOUSE, KITCHEN   99

       Andy walks in. Marva hands Andy a stack of messages. Gene
       folds down his paper to look at Andy who gives a half-baked
       smile.

100   EXT. TAGGERT HOUSE, DRIVEWAY   100

       Andy drives off in the truck. Gene watches proudly.

101   EXT. SIX DIFFERENT HOUSES - DAY   101

       Match Cut: Andy's van is parked in front of different homes.

102   INT. SIX DIFFERENT HOUSES, LIVING ROOMS - DAY   102

       Different COUPLES sit on different couches in different
       living rooms. Andy sitting across from them, listening to
       these various stories.

BREAKING DOWN SAMPLE FEATURE FILM SIDE #1

I have very fond memories of this audition scene. This is from the feature film "Valley of the Sun" which was directed by Stokes McIntyre and Christopher Hall. The actors were brought in individually for the role of Mr. Smith. I asked to see their own interpretation of the scene and they actually got to audition with the director of this movie that day. The actor that was chosen did the most amazing read. It brought tears to my eyes and I was in awe of his ability to create magic out of these lines. He was a very special man by the name of Phillip Thorneycroft and had amazing gifts as an actor. He ended up passing away about 2 years ago and he is truly missed by all of us here in Arizona.

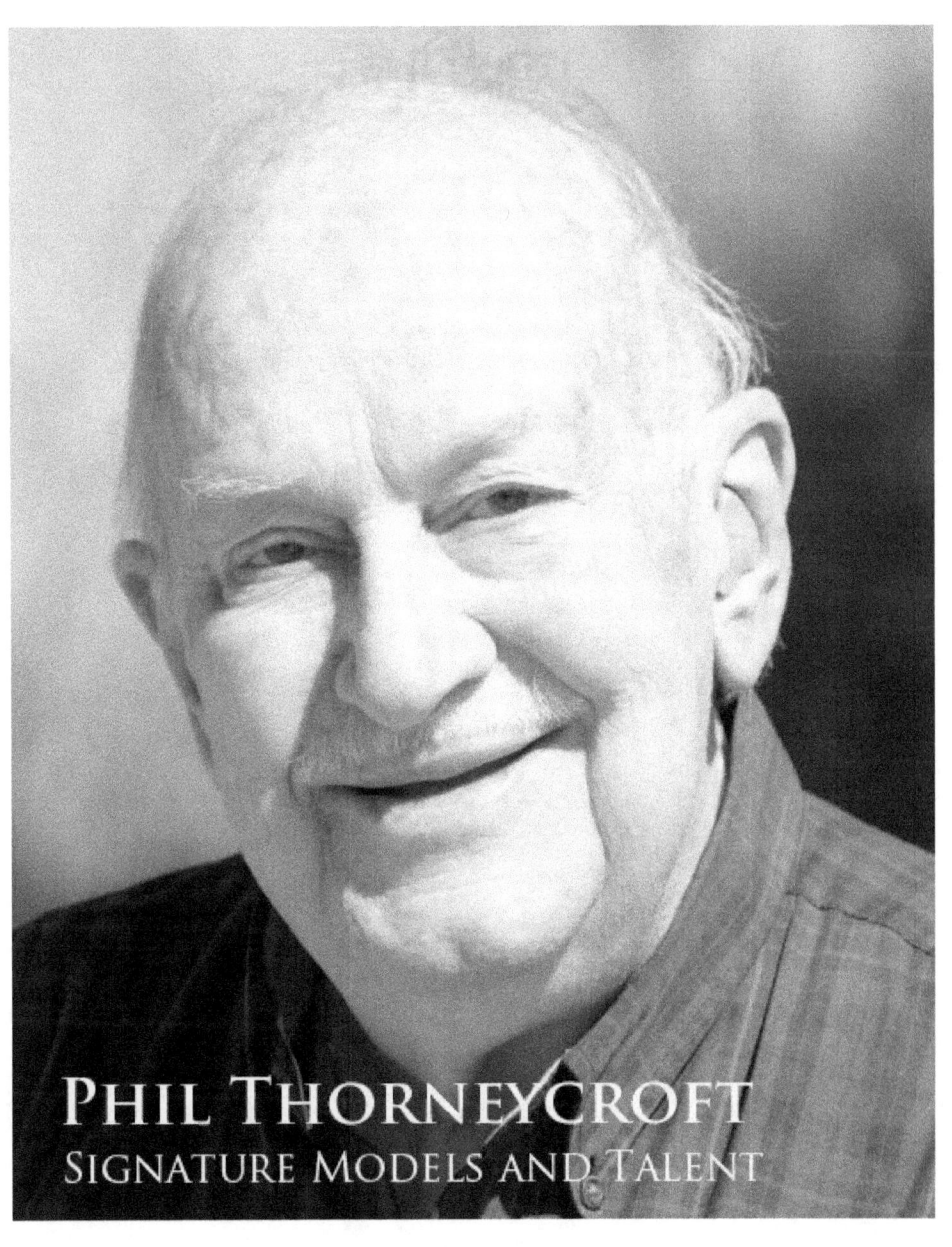

PHIL THORNEYCROFT
SIGNATURE MODELS AND TALENT

SAMPLE FEATURE FILM SIDE #2

                    JOLENE (CONT'D)
          You can't even play a Bobbie Gentry
          record past 10pm without someone
          pounding on your floor with a
          broom. Although I'll take this
          place any day over what I was
          dealing with at Rance's McMansion.

Both women laugh.

                    JOLENE (CONT'D)
          Rance left a message on my cell
          phone crying and apologizing and he
          mentioned Bobby split town. I think
          he went back east.

                    CARRIE-ANN
          Do you think he went back east in
          the present time or back east in
          1957?

The woman laugh harder.

Jolene hops the fence of the padlocked pool gate then helps
Carrie-Anne over.

                    CARRIE-ANNE
          I ain't never been skinny dipping
          before

                    JOLENE
          Too shy?

                    CARRIE-ANNE
          Nah. I'm in. Let's try it.

Carrie-Anne slowly takes off her clothes but leaves on her
underwear. Jolene takes everything off. They take off their
clothes slowly, thinking that whipping them off will make
more noise in the apartment complex. It makes them seem like
an older married couple, meticulously taking their clothes
off to go to bed. As they submerge their bodies in the pool
the coldness of the water startles them but they continue to
ease up. Carrie-Anne only then elects to take off her bra and
panties while fully underwater.

                    JOLENE
          Why Carrie-Anne Edwards, you are a
          prude!

Carrie-Anne giggles. They move closer to each other and begin
line dancing in the water, repeating many of the same moves.
At one point they come face to face and really look at each
other. Uncomfortable silence follows.

                    CARRIE-ANNE
          I'm scared. I'm scared to look at
          you too close.

                    JOLENE
          I'm scared too.

                    CARRIE-ANNE
          What are you scared about?

                    JOLENE
          I'm scared that I've only been so
          entranced with what I look like
          that if I see myself, really see
          myself in someone else, I'm not
          gonna like what I see. What about
          you?

                    CARRIE-ANNE
          I'm scared about wanting something
          really bad, finally admitting it
          out loud and then having it pull
          away. I keep having this nightmare
          of being shipwrecked on an island,
          sleeping on a shore and seeing the
          rescue boat at the horizon, sailing
          away for home, not seeing me jump
          up and down saying, "I'm here, I'm
          here."

Carrie-Ann starts tearing up. It has Jolene shook up.

More silence and staring.

                    JOLENE
          Well, by my count, no one's pulling
          away in horror.

                    CARRIE-ANNE
          So...is this it? The something I've
          always feared not happening...
          happening?

                    JOLENE
          Yeah, it is.

                    CARRIE-ANNE
          Like, tomorrow when we wake up, is
          the water going to suddenly circle
          down the drain counter clockwise or
          something? And is the sun going to
          set in the east but only for us?

Jolene bends over and reaches into the mini bar and grabs a
wine cooler.

Breaking down sample feature film side #2

This script is from a movie called Queens of Country which was directed by Ryan Page and Christopher Pomerenke. It was a comedy and starred Ron Livingston, Lizzie Caplain and Joe Lo Truglio. I brought in a hand full of females to audition for the role of Carrie-Ann. This was a body double role and we had to match up females that resembled Lizzie Caplain. Lizzy plays Jolene a female that realizes she is in love with herself and her alter personality "Carrie-Ann".

SAMPLE COMMERCIAL SCRIPT #1

GDP: The Quiz :30
6.22.10

INT. Day. Go Daddy Call Center. An attractive female call center employee, Jane takes a customer call.

JANE
Thanks for calling GoDaddy.com. This is Jane. How can I...

Cut to a middle-aged man, Ralph, in what appears to be a home office. He seems just a little surprised by the voice on the other end of the phone. He interrupts.

RALPH
Jane, eh? What's your real name?

Cut back to Jane. She's unfazed by the question.

JANE
My real name is Jane, Sir

Ralph interrupts.

RALPH
Riiight. I guess you'd also like me to believe you're here in America?

Jane smiles as if she's been down this road before.

JANE
All GoDaddy.com customer service is based right here in the USA!

Ralph is still suspicious. What follows is a series of rapid-fire questions.

RALPH
That right, Jane? First President?

JANE
George Washington

RALPH
Vice President?

JANE
John Adams

RALPH
Capital of Texas?

JANE
Austin
RALPH
Who won the 1994 World Series?

JANE
Trick question. There was no winner.

RALPH

Impressive.

JANE
Thanks, Now, I have a question for you.

RALPH
Shoot

JANE
How can I help with your domain and website?

Ralph smiles. Cut to tag.

ANNC
Go Daddy.com. USA-based customer service...domains,
websites and everything in between.

BREAKING DOWN SAMPLE COMMERCIAL SCRIPT #1

In the script you just read, both the male and female roles were to be cast. Males and females were paired up and brought in together. Although the characters are in separate locations in the script, for the audition, a table with two chairs had the actors sit side by side. I directed them to face outwards towards the camera during their reading together. The female was given a headset, as if she was at an office call center and the male was told to sit comfortably in a chair as if he was at work.

As this commercial has a very light-hearted feel, the actors were directed to keep in mind that the question/answer scenario needed to be done with humor. The italicized stage directions allow the actor to understand where the director is going with the character's emotions. After the questioning by Ralph (about where Jane is really located), Jane brought us back to the original reason why Ralph was calling, which demonstrates, to the target audience, that Go Daddy is a USA product and its customer service base is located right here in the good ol' USA.

SAMPLE COMMERCIAL SCRIPT #2

Copy Proof Version: 3
Title: "FRANK"
Project: VQC22544_NewBranding_TV
Date: 2/25/11

Concept: FRANK, a regular guy in his mid-forties, talks to camera as he walks from the Blackjack table to the Players Club. He's interrupted by people he knows as he makes his way across the crowded casino floor.

SFX: Ambient casino noises

FRANK
For me, the reason I come to Vee Quiva Casino is because...

Frank picks up his chips, tips the dealer and starts walking.

DEALER
(OS) Thank you, Frank.

He nods to the dealer and keeps walking.

FRANK
(to Dealer) No, thank you.
(to Camera) is because they...

WOMAN
(OS) You were right about this machine!

94

Woman off-screen interrupts Frank. He steps over to high-five her at her slot machine. He continues walking and talking towards camera.

FRANK
(to Woman) It's my favorite...
(to camera) So what I love about...

PLAYERS CLUB REP
Hi Frank

He acknowledges the Players Club representative and turns to the camera with a smile...

FRANK
(to PC Rep) Hi Anne.
(to Camera) ...it's my place to play!

Cut to quick shots like: A group cheers at a Bingo table. A waitress delivers a drink. Two friends hug at a slot machine. The Gils River Riches Meter climbs. A guy playing poker scoops up chips.

Fade to Vee Quiva logo. The words "West Valley's" fly in and land on top of the logo.

SUPER
"Your place to play – Minutes Away"

BREAKING DOWN SAMPLE
COMMERCIAL SCRIPT #2

In this example, note the date the script was approved and also the revision number. This script is separated into the "audio" (what we hear) and "video" (what we see). I auditioned several males for the role of Frank. During the audition, the actor was asked to walk slowly from the back of the room and say his lines to camera. He needed to use strong active visuals (in his mind) to portray making his way through the casino and interacting with the people in the script. A lot of direction is thrown at him in the "video" section, which is not easy.

It is like the old game we played, as kids, rubbing our bellies while patting our heads. Not only must Frank be in sync with the lines and action at the same time, but also interact with his "friends" and respond to what they are saying to him.

The commercial ends with Frank telling us, "It's my place to play." Thus, a sense of community and family is demonstrated with very few words.

SAMPLE COMMERCIAL SCRIPT #3

Air Marketing
TV Title: Playoff
Length: :30

Open on the interior of a Peter Piper Pizza restaurant. It is lively, and we see people eating at tables in the dining room, and playing and enjoying the game room. We see a family near the hoops game, the kids are playing against the parents. The kids have a long line of tickets coming from their game, the parents lag behind.

SUPER: A Pie Chart is onscreen with two sections that are acting as a score keeper between "Kids" and "Parents". The kids section is larger and growing.

We see one of the kids nail a shot, and a few more tickets are added to their pile.

SUPER: The "Kids" section of the Pie Chart grows even more.

Dad hands the ball to Mom as she steps in for her turn. We see several quick cuts of swish after swish. Tickets continue to flow.

SUPER: The Pie Chart changes with each cut to reflect Mom's hoops dominance, until finally the "Parents" section is ¾ of the Pie.

The kids look at the Pie Chart scoreboard, dejected until the "Parents" section disappears altogether leaving only

"Kids". Mom hands them all her tickets and the kids are relieved to have won after all.

AVO: At Peter Piper Pizza, we shoot to bring out the best in family completion. The results...may surprise you!

Food/Bundle Imagery and AVO

ART CARD: Logo, tag and URL up.

AVO: Peter Piper Pizza. Everyone grab a slice.

BREAKING DOWN SAMPLE COMMERCIAL SCRIPT #3

This is a non-speaking commercial: no lines for the actors, only actions and reactions. Although this may seem easy, it is a challenge! When you see the word *Super*, a superimposed graphic is indicated, which is treated the same as any product, person or detail. The eventual position of the *super* in the frame may cause you to sit, stand or move in a certain way to create room for it to be placed in postproduction. In the audition, you *do not* have to be concerned with the super.

For this audition, a mom, a dad and two kids were brought in together. They all stood and faced the camera, using wadded paper to recreate little basketballs, then ran through the action, interacting with each other and the game. During non-speaking auditions, we prefer the actors use their eyes and facial expressions, only, to portray their character. Many times, actors want to talk and improvise, but this is not recommended. Some directors insist the actors do not say a word and use facial expressions only to get their point across. Feel free to ask whether you can speak out loud, before the audition begins.

Peter Piper Pizza commercials are notorious for using little vignettes to sell their product. It is not only about the food, as you can see, but also about the fun, entertainment and bonding with friends and family. These are always enjoyable commercials to be a part of. The kids are very important, and the chemistry of the family plays a big role in the casting process. Also vital is the look of everyone. The ad agency and client emphasize matching up the right looks to make their "families." Many times, with families we have certain ones that really stand out above the rest. I may see a very natural performance from the mom and son, but the sister is like a deer in headlights. This tells us she will not do well on set in this situation.

Sample commercial script #4

Length: 30 TV

VIRAL SPOTS

"Travel agent"

OPEN INSIDE OZZIE'S OFFICE. WE SEE AN UNUSUAL NUMBER OF VACATION POSTERS ON THE WALL AND A SIGN THAT READS, "Dream vacations."

Ozzie: Where do you wanna go?

Man: It's our honeymoon. We're thinking Paris.

Ozzie: No. Venezuela. It's like heaven. And you can get some sun on your pale skin.

Man: But we really had our hearts set on...

Ozzie: What are you gonna do in Paris? See some museums? You can do that in Venezuela.

Man: Yeah but...

Ozzie: Relaxing on beautiful beaches, drinking Pina Coladas all day.

Man: Maybe I should just...

Ozzie: Say Pina Colada.

Man: Pina Colada.

OZZIE PICKS UP THE PHONE AND STARTS DIALING.

Ozzie: You're going to Venezuela.

Title: Life isn't black & white. Baseball should be.

CUT TO TITLE W/LOGO

Title: Season tickets on sale now.

Breaking down sample commercial script #4

This commercial's appeal depends upon knowledge of the former White Sox coach Ozzie Guillen. I directed the actors to use the camera lens for "Ozzie" and to speak and react directly to camera. They auditioned alone not with the actual Ozzie Guillen. The actor read the lines for "Man" but not much direction was provided in the script, so I left it up to the actor to bring his own personality to the read. I then requested a different interpretation from the actors so that I could see their range.

Sample commercial storyboard #1

Client: Cable ONE CAB_691
Length: 30 TV
Title: "Tool Belt"
Date: 12-08-08

OPEN ON WIFE AS SHE
PLACES CABLE ONE MODEM
BOX ON TABLE.

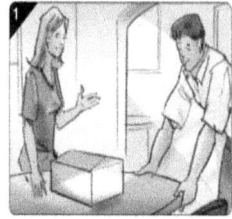

MUSIC UNDER:

JIM:
Cable ONE High Speed Internet.

CUT TO HUSBAND TAKING
MODEM OUT OF BOX.

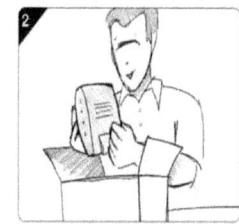

Sweeeeet!

WIFE LOOKING AT CABLES.

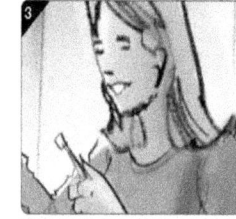

SHARON:
Think it'll be hard to hook up?

CUT TO HUSBAND TURNING
HIS BACK AND SYMBOLICALLY
ROLLING UP HIS SLEEVES.

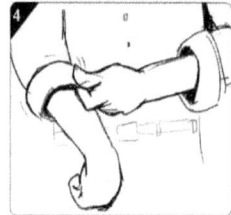

JIM:
(TIM ALLEN-ESQUE)
Whew, probably gonna need
some extra cable.

POV INSIDE CLOSET AS HE
OPENS DOORS.

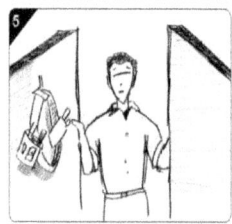

Maybe an Allen Wrench...

Client: Cable ONE CAB_691
Length: 30 TV
Title: "Tool Belt"
Date: 12-08-08

HAND GRABS TOOL BELT

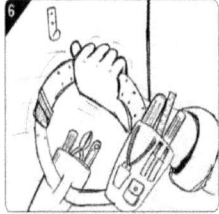

But don't worry.

SHE EXAMINES CABLES

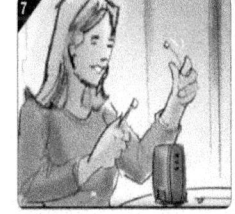

(BEAT)

MATCH CLICKING OF TOOL
BELT...

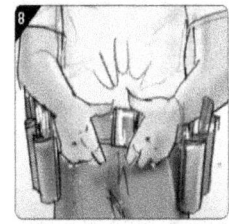

I can handle it.

TO WIFE CLICKING IN FIRST
CABLE...

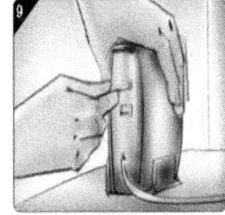

ANNCR:
The fact is, anybody can.

TO SLIDING SCREW-DRIVER
INTO TOOL BELT...

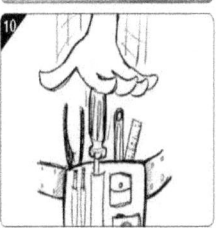

(BEAT)

Client: Cable ONE CAB_691
Length: 30 TV
Title: "Tool Belt"
Date: 12-08-08

CLICKING SECOND CABLE...

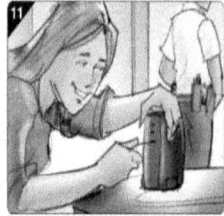

Just a few quick, clicks and
you're online

AND TURNING COMPUTER ON.

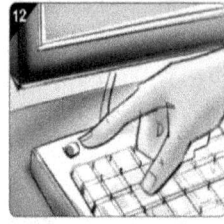

SFX:
(COMPUTER START-UP CHIME)

with the fastest internet
connection there is.

HE HEARS SOUND AND TURNS
TO COMPUTER. HE SUDDENLY
REALIZES THAT HIS WIFE HAS
BEATEN HIM TO IT.

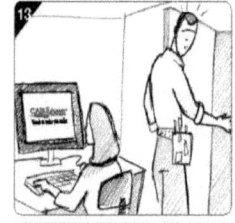

JIM:
(WOUNDED PRIDE)
Y'know, I could have done it.

SHE GIVES HIM A PLAYFUL SHOT
IN THE ARM.

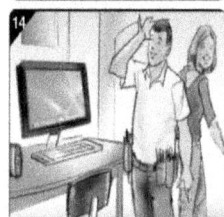

SHARON:
(PROUD OF HERSELF)
I know.

HE PLOPS DOWN AND SITS ON
A SHARP TOOL. THEN TURNS TO
MONITOR.

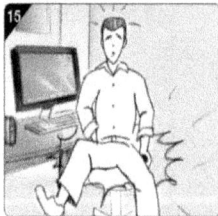

JIM:
OUCH!

ANNCR:
Cable ONE High Speed Internet.

Client: Cable ONE CAB_691
Length: 30 TV
Title: "Tool Belt"
Date: 12-08-08

CUT TO TIGHT SHOT OF
UNNECESSARY TOOL BELT.

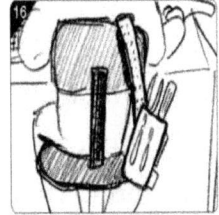

It's as easy to install as it is to use.

PAN UP TO SHOW HIM
HAPPILY ONLINE.

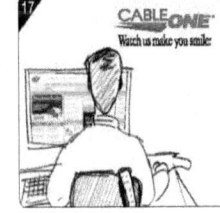

SONG:
Watch us make you smile.

BREAKING DOWN STORYBOARD #1

As you can see, the storyboard has photos depicting the actors' actions, facial expressions and movements. The audio is underlined on the right, so it stands out. The stage direction and camera angles appear on the left. The characters are "Jim" and "Sharon." For this audition, couples were brought in together, to see their chemistry. They were told to keep it playful and lighthearted. We had a tool belt prop for Jim to use and a simple table, chair and computer prop.

I must poke fun at this casting, because it does show the feminization of our males. Many commercials we see these days are geared towards the female taking over the male roles in the household. I call this female the "alpha male" and I call the males "half stupid".

Some auditions have a storyboard for you to study, but many do not. Treat storyboards as you would a script and use them to your benefit, utilizing the generous amount of information and pictures.

Finished Products

I enjoy watching the finished products of some of the films and commercials I have worked on. I have included links to the feature film trailers as well as some of the commercials of the scripts included in this book. The actors are all believable and natural and that is why they were chosen. Type the URL into your web browser's address bar to see the results.

Valley of the Sun feature film

To view the movie trailer, go to: https://www.youtube.com/watch?v=kQ32fVdYjnc

Queens of Country feature film

To view the movie trailer, go to: https://www.youtube.com/watch?v=CjwSYnXaAK0

Go Daddy "Quiz" commercial

To view the actual commercial, go to: http://www.youtube.com/watch?v=ISvPqixjrps

Vee Quiva Casino commercial

To view the actual commercial, go to:

http://www.youtube.com/watch?v=b-4knJiPBj4

Peter Piper Pizza commercial

To view the actual commercial, go to:
http://www.youtube.com/watch?v=D4dY-An1LIU

Cable One Storyboard

To view the actual commercial, go to:
http://www.youtube.com/watch?v=ahrrcgOtE6Y

SUMMARY: ANALYZING SCRIPTS

1. Break down the script into a beginning, middle and ending.
2. Ask yourself questions like: *Who am I talking to? What is the conflict/resolution? Where am I? Who is my target audience?*
3. Divide the script into distinct emotional changes.
4. Make strong, but smooth, transitions throughout the script.
5. Keep your performance real.
6. Practice out loud and with a family member or friend.
7. Be careful not to over rehearse your lines.
8. Always bring *yourself* to the character.

CHAPTER 11

PREPARING FOR YOUR PERFORMANCE

I can usually spot an inexperienced actor the moment they walk into the room. Occasionally, someone fools me and can pull off an audition, only to tell me at the end that it was their first time. *Inexperienced* actors tend to either make bland, boring choices or overact their lines. Many are just not prepared. There is so much more to acting than learning lines, as you will see in this next chapter.

BEING REAL

"Being real" is the name of the game in acting. This was a concept I was not aware of, until I started handling auditions. I began to see and learn the difference between a really good performance and an over acted one. Directors love it when the actor appears to not actually be "acting" and are just "being real".

Being real are two words that are repeated, again and again, like a mantra, by directors and creative advertising people. They are looking for naturalness not forced or fake performances. Remember they want to connect with people, not actors!

With all auditions, we do not want to see you playing a character. You will merge and adapt the character to you. In other words, play yourself! Meaning yourself as if you had those personality traits or what I like to think of as "putting *yourself* in the characters shoes". If you are playing a doctor…how would you be as an actual doctor if you did the schooling etc. This is a good place to start but always keep in mind the doctor may be played as a complete opposite of you. You will learn to adapt and to elicit those emotions needed.

LEARNING YOUR LINES

Now that you've got your script, you need to prepare for your audition. It is important to try to memorize your lines so well; you could say them in your sleep. Say them out loud, practice them with someone else; do your homework until you know your lines. Do not add your own dialogue or lines to the script. Take your script with you to the audition to use as a reference. Do not stress if it is a larger script and you have trouble memorizing all the lines...do the best you can. Many times, clients put unnecessary pressure on the actors because they did not send out the script until the night before the audition. Many actors have other jobs to contend with!

If you have a video recorder put yourself on tape performing your lines. You will learn a lot from watching yourself during playback. This is a great way to see the reality of how you look on camera which you may not like at first, but after practicing and performing again and again you may discover that "wow! I look and sound really believable in this role!"

COLD READ AUDITION

A cold read is an audition with a script in hand: you will not have had the lines to memorize beforehand. One way to prepare for a cold read is to practice reading out loud from a magazine or book, holding it low and slightly off to the side of your face. You will look and feel awkward at first while trying to remain believable and natural. The ideal way to learn the skill of cold reading is to take a class or workshop that focuses on cold reading techniques. Do not keep your face in the page. Remember to act, react and be natural. As you go along you can look down and get your line in your mind and then look up and deliver it.

When you are at the audition, quickly analyze the piece first, to decide where to make your choices for your character. Believable choices (strong, laid back, aggressive, etc..) are *always* better than boring and bland choices. While you are waiting to audition, find a quiet space to be able to practice the lines out loud. Trust your instincts to mold the character to you.

MORE THAN ONE ACTOR

Auditioning with other people in the scene is even trickier. Too many times, actors who have memorized their own lines, have no idea where their lines occur during the dialogue; they do not have the timing of their own lines down. This will ensure you *do not* get the job.

You will need to familiarize yourself with the other characters lines. Not knowing the timing of your own lines will throw the entire audition off and the other actors will be irritated that they were paired with you. I have seen this again and again! If you have time...learn all the lines in the scenes.

REACTING TO OTHERS

You probably know someone, whether family members, friends or maybe even your spouse, that does not listen to you when you speak because they are too concerned with what they are going to say. They may even interrupt you to get their point across. They listen with their mouths not their ears! Talk about frustrating! This is a *huge* problem in the audition room as well! Actors that are too busy thinking about their own lines (trust me this shows on their face) or looking down at the script reading along, rather than *listening* and *reacting* to the dialogue given by the other actor(s). You may have heard the saying, "acting is reacting," and it is very true. Being able to *hear* the words spoken by the other actors and react to them is *just as* important as delivering your own lines in a believable and natural way. *Do not* look at your lines while the other actor is speaking... *listen and react*! We may just have the camera pointed at you. *Do not* exaggerate your facial expressions...think it and feel it and we will see it. Once again...we may have the camera pointing at you to see you reacting to the other actors!

If you need to, *after* another actor has said his lines and you have listened and reacted, look down at the script and get your next line. Of course, *always* look up and out to the camera to deliver it.

The other person may be a bad actor (for instance the casting director herself) but don't let this affect you. Commit to how you rehearsed it and go at your own pace unless directed otherwise. We will quickly see that you do not have a problem. If you feel rushed or cannot hear your cues, ask them nicely to slow it down at first.

MONOLOGUE AUDITION

In a monologue audition, you will provide the monologue, not the client, as it is a pre-rehearsed audition piece that suites you personally. Monologue auditions allow you to control your audition. A monologue is a scene with you as the only actor in it. It is like having a good conversation with a close friend. Be sure to have your monologue completely memorized! Also, be sure to have the type of monologue that has been requested. It is best to prepare a comedic and a dramatic monologue to have ready to perform at any time. Many websites and books can assist you to find the right monologue. Keep away from TV shows and popular movies, so that you are not compared to the original actor who popularized the role.

PERSONALITY AUDITION

Usually, you will be asked your name and a little bit about yourself. Do not treat this like a job interview. Talking about how bad you want to be an actor (duh you are at the audition and we know this!) and listing your credits is *not* what we are looking for.... boring! We do not care about your credits; we want to see your personality. We want to see that you have a sense of humor. Many times, I like to throw in strange questions like, "if you could be a superhero, who would you be and why?" or "what is the one thing you could not live without and why?" or "who do you take after the most in your family and why?" If you give us one-word responses, we will say "Next!" So just have fun and let your personality show!

SUMMARY: PREPARING FOR YOUR PERFORMANCE

1. Learn to "be real" and be yourself.
2. Try to memorize the lines to the best of your ability; never add your own words to the script.
3. Practice for cold readings by reading out loud from a magazine or book. Better yet...sign up for a cold reading workshop.
4. Do not look down while reading; rather, look up after you have your line say it with your head up (or out of the page), as if talking to someone.
5. If auditioning with other actors, always know where your lines come in.
6. Always react to the other actors and do not look down at your script while they are doing their lines. Acting is reacting.
7. Prepare a comedic and dramatic monologue, which should be well rehearsed. Once again, keep the dialogue conversational, as if talking to a friend.
8. Always give more than one-word answers during personality interviews. Be sure to show your personality and do not talk about acting or list your credits.

CHAPTER 12

WHAT TO BRING TO YOUR AUDITION

Time and again, actors show up unprepared and without their tools. I am not referring to your screwdrivers and a hammer. Your tools are what we refer to in the industry as your "calling card" and are expected at every audition. You will appear to be unprofessional if you do not have the following items. Keep in mind the casting director may not request all of them but better to have them just in case.

HEADSHOT

There are a couple of different types of headshots used in the industry. The main ones are a commercial headshot and theatrical headshot. A good commercial headshot should show plenty of teeth. The smile should be big and bright, and your eyes need to smile too. You should look happy, warm and approachable. A theatrical headshot is more common with film auditions. You may have a serious or contemplative look or even a slight smile. I highly recommend your headshot is in color. Black and white headshots are outdated now. It is also important that your headshot is not cropped tight, meaning we do not want to see a big head on the paper. You can even show your body from the waist up which we refer to as a three-quarter shot or loose headshot.

Composites (where you have a larger photo on front and several smaller pictures on the back) used to be popular but now are mostly used by models. Stick to the standard 8 x 10 or 8 ½ x 11 headshots for film and commercial auditions. Your headshot, not a highly edited glamour shot, will show you, wrinkles and all. What a disappointment to request an actor based on his headshot, only to have him show up, looking nothing like the picture! *See sample headshots at the end of this chapter.*

At a recent casting for a large national commercial I selected an older actor from his headshot and invited him to the audition. He had a great character look in his photos with good energy in his eyes and I was very excited to meet him. Remember I am looking for solutions to my problems and I thought for sure he would be it. When he showed up at the audition, he had had so much plastic surgery since that photo was taken that he could barely close his lips around his teeth! He looked like he belonged in the National Inquirer. I could not concentrate on his performance and was instead freaked out by the changes in his appearance and bummed that my search was still on.

You should update your headshot as you age and change your look. Do not use headshots from when you were younger (very popular), thinner (very popular), had longer hair, etc. It is your responsibility to look like your current headshot. Get professional headshots, if you plan on being more involved in the industry. You can also find a less experienced photographer who is willing to trade time and prints (or digital images) with you. This also helps build their portfolio. (Just be careful females as they may want to sleep with you too!). Watch your drinks ladies and men when out with photographers you just met. We do not want to see you roofied! These things do happen!

Color headshots are once again the preferred standard. Once you get your great headshot you can then have high quality low-cost reproductions made of it and there are several online companies that offer this service.

Models have a habit of bringing in their portfolios. These are *huge* books they must carry around for their modeling calls that are actually bigger than some of the models carrying them. We do not have the time or desk space to go through these. Leave these for the modeling calls not the film or commercial auditions.

RESUME

Print out a simple resume, showing your name, height, weight, eye color, hair color and contact phone number, agent info (if you have one) and then, list your experience or training (if any). List your special skills at the bottom. *See the sample resume at the end of this chapter.*

Many actors keep copies of their headshot and resume in their car always in case there is a last-minute audition. Always staple your headshot and resume, back to back, before coming to the audition!

SCRIPT/PEN

Bring your script with you to the audition. Also, bring a pen and highlighter just in case it is a cold read which will allow you to make your lines stand out while preparing.

PROPS

Do not bring props unless asked. We may provide props at the casting for you. When casting athletes, for example, I may ask the actors to bring their own golf club or sports equipment, etc.

WHO TO BRING TO YOUR AUDITION

Most casting facilities are not very large in size, so waiting room space is limited. If you are taking your minor child, one parent is enough: Do not bring the whole family including grandma and Skippy the dog to wait with you. Rather, have them wait outside, in the car or at a nearby coffee shop. Otherwise, they are taking chairs from other actors. If you are an adult, it is best to arrive by yourself and have your spouse, friend, mom, boyfriend (I could go into a whole chapter here but will leave that to my next book. "Jealous Boyfriends and how to maneuver them out of your acting universe"), wait outside.

The only exception to this is when you are not comfortable with the audition location or know very little about who you are meeting. Your safety comes first, and there can be some sketchy types who pretend to be someone they are not. This happens a lot more with pretty females so beware of modeling calls in private hotel rooms. I encountered this when younger. I received a call from a so-called "director" for a print shoot audition and went to a hotel to meet him and his "staff". I ended up receiving an offer to fly over seas but luckily the night before I was slated to fly out a friend called and said she knew someone dealing with this same person and we both realized that we would have ended up in the sex trade industry! So many red flags but I was young and did not heed the warning signs that were staring me in the face. Once again…you can get roofied at an audition (given a date rape drug called GHB). Hotel room auditions can be sketchy unless held in the lobby area or ballroom area. I am also hearing more and more that this is happening in the sex cam industry as well. People place ads for sex models etc. and request you come to do a shoot in a hotel room all expenses paid. It appears to be on the up and up but if you are roofied, they can film you while doing heinous acts to you and sell this online and you have no idea this happened!

NOURISHMENT

Just in case the audition is running late, bring a bottle of water. It is also a good idea to have a very light snack on hand. You may be missing lunch to do the audition and you will want to have your energy up and something in your stomach, so you can focus on your read and not your hunger. This is especially true for kids: please feed them before the audition and/or have a snack for them to eat during their wait. People with health issues such as diabetes should most definitely bring a snack or insulin or medication for their health issue. I had an actor show up for an audition and while waiting to come in he went into a diabetic coma and we had to scramble to find him something to eat. Talk about delaying the audition!

SAMPLE RESUME

Linda Turner

222-222-2222

(Agent Name, Phone, Email)

Height: 5'7"
Weight: 130
Hair: Brown
Eyes: Brown

FILM

Yesterday's Tomorrow	Featured	Channel Zero Productions

COMMERCIAL

Resort Quest	Principal	Oceanic Cable 16
Wisk Laundry Detergent	Principal	Alcone Marketing Group
Pontiac	Featured	MacLaren McCann Canada
Oasis Water Park	Principal	Pointe South Mountain

THEATRE

Miracle Worker	Helen Keller	Tampa Theatre Works

INTERNET

Discount Cab	Principal	Cox Media

PRINT

Sheraton Resort	Principal	Deutsche

TRAINING

Commercial Acting		The Acting Connection
Scene Study		John Benton

SPECIAL SKILLS

Dance (ballet, jazz), horseback riding, tennis, softball, yoga, computers, school teacher

SAMPLE HEADSHOTS

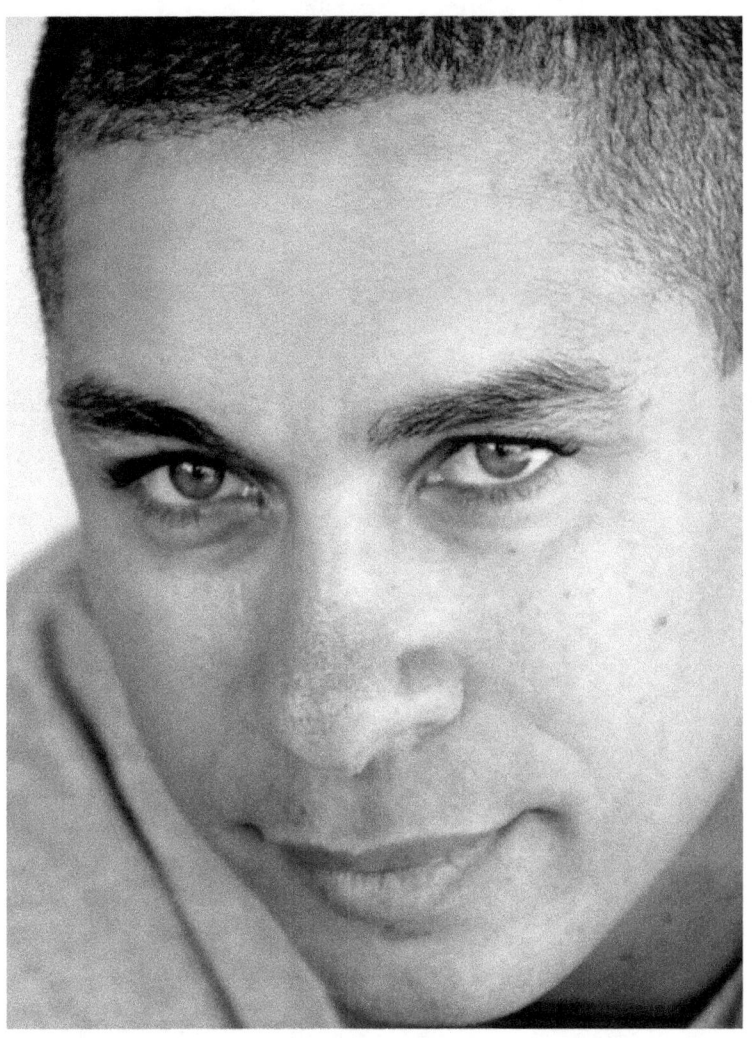

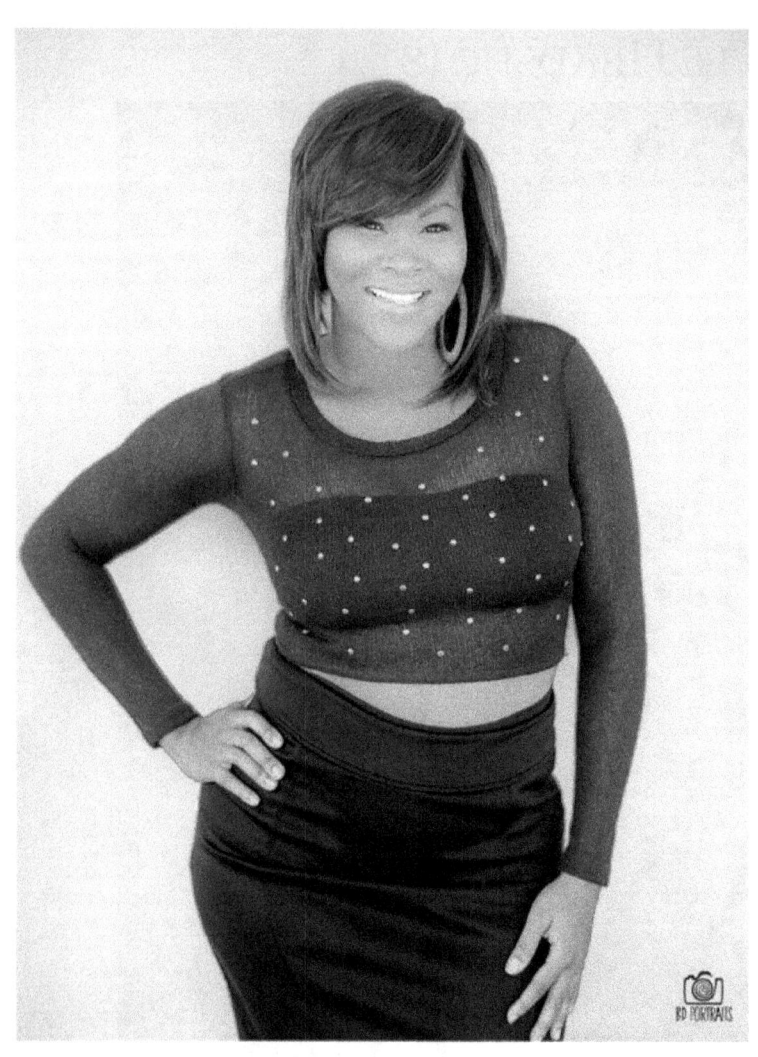

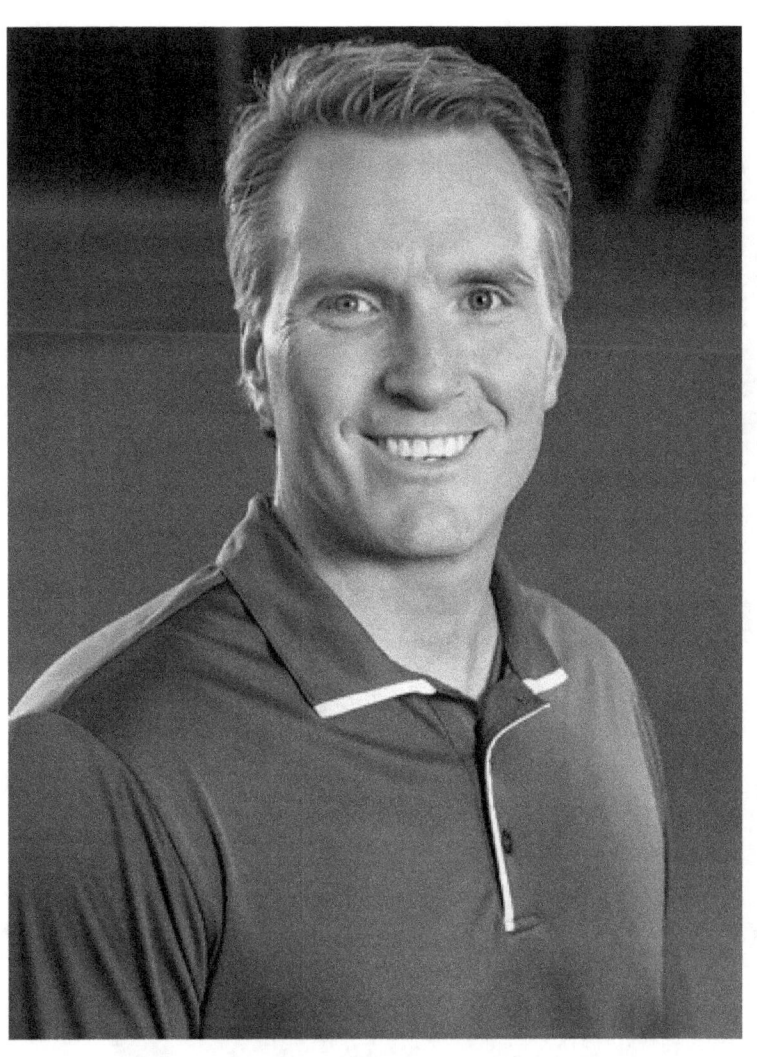

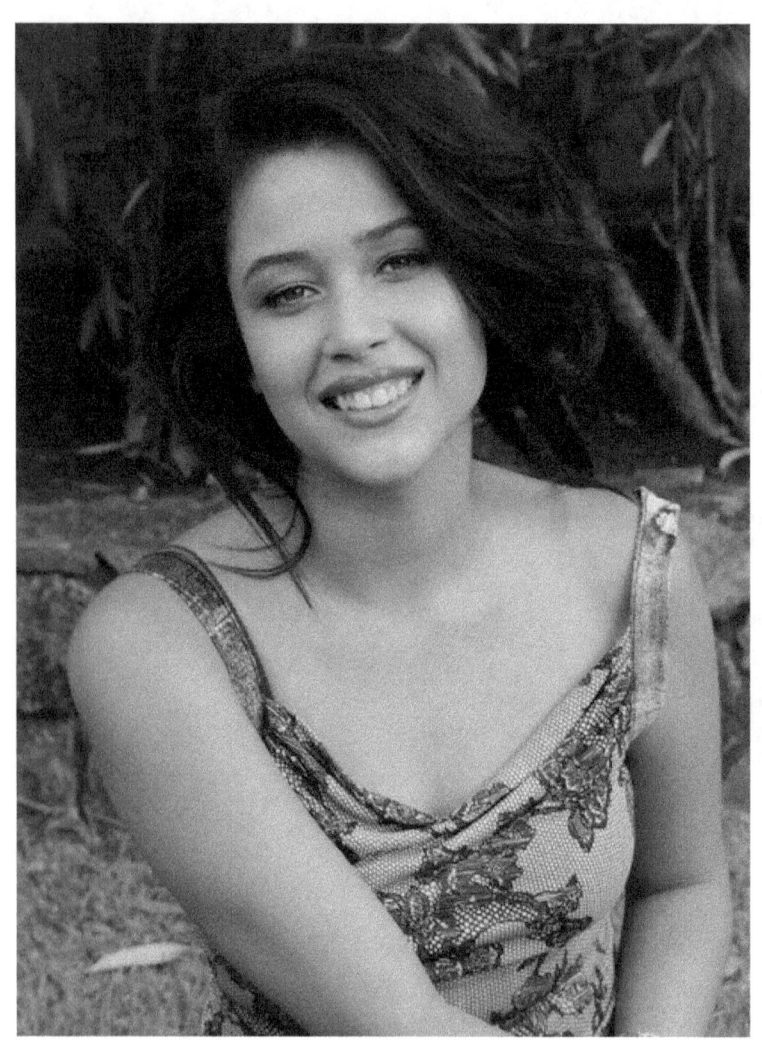

134

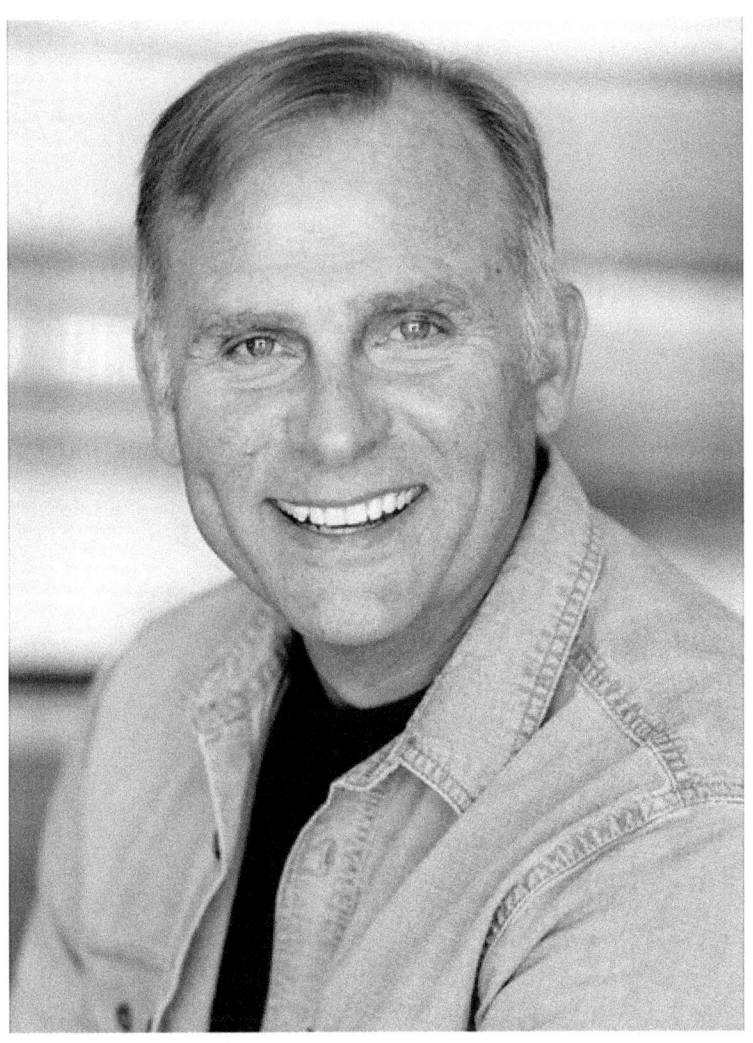

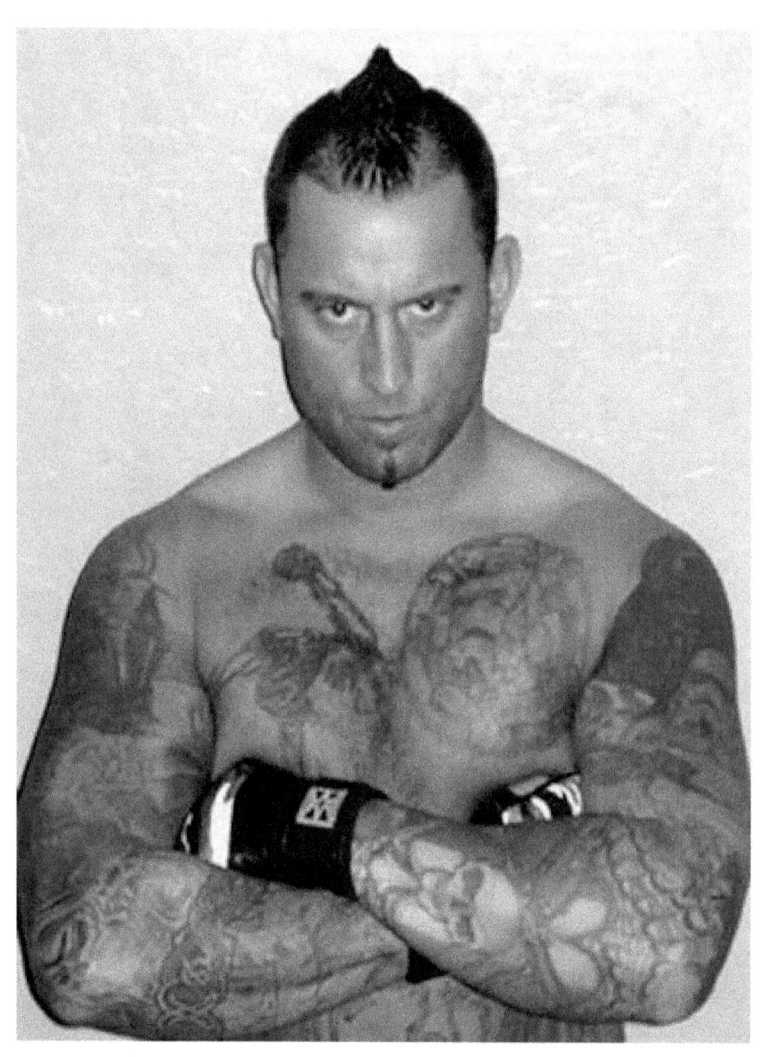

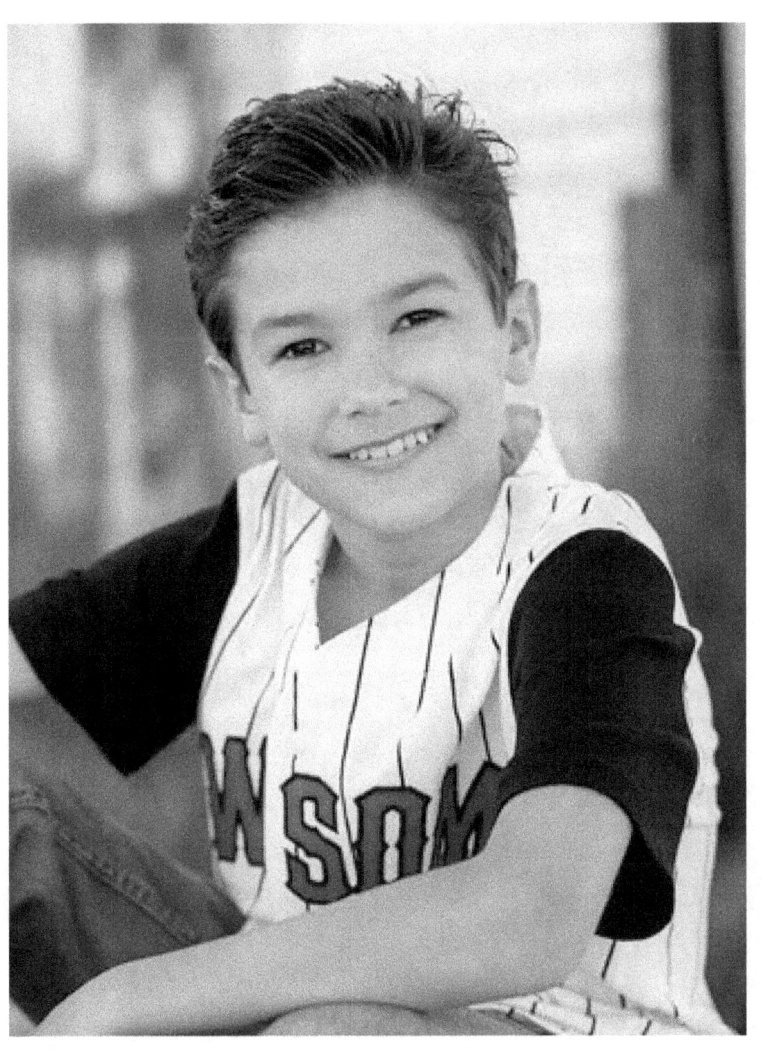

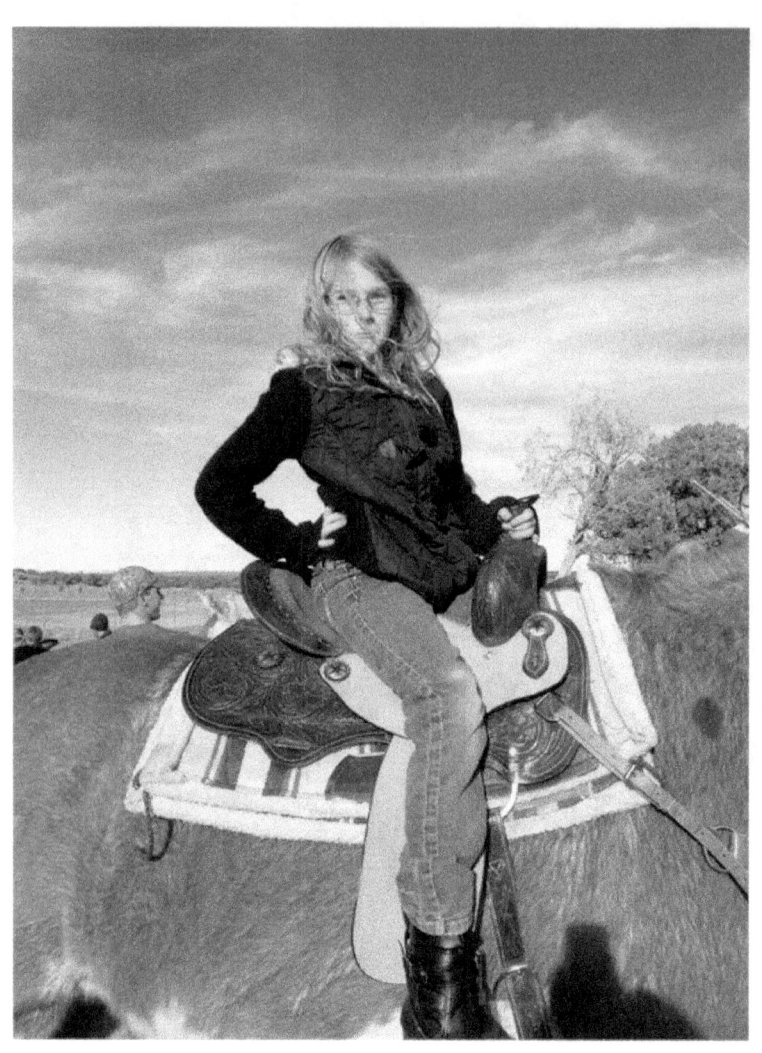

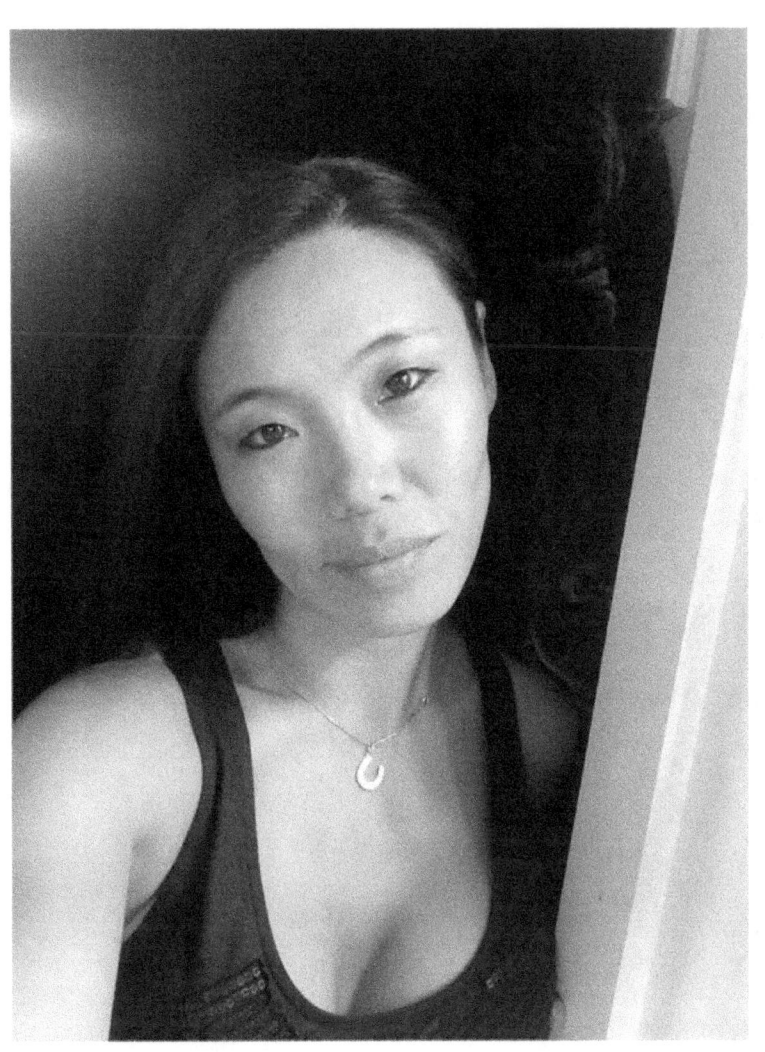

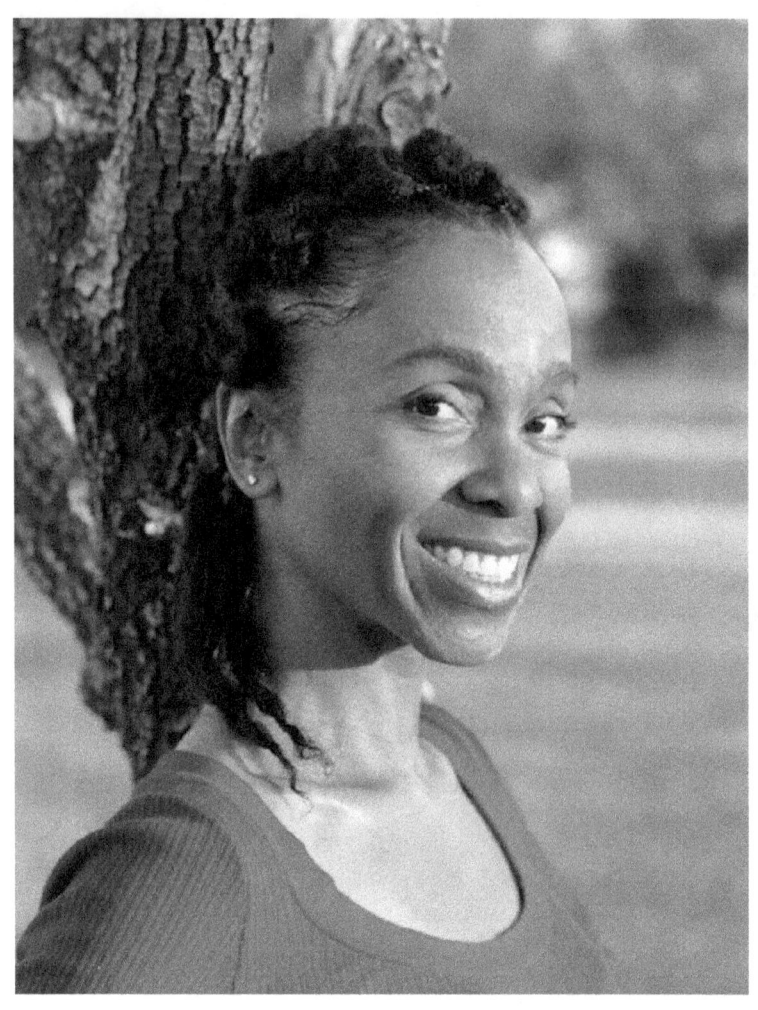

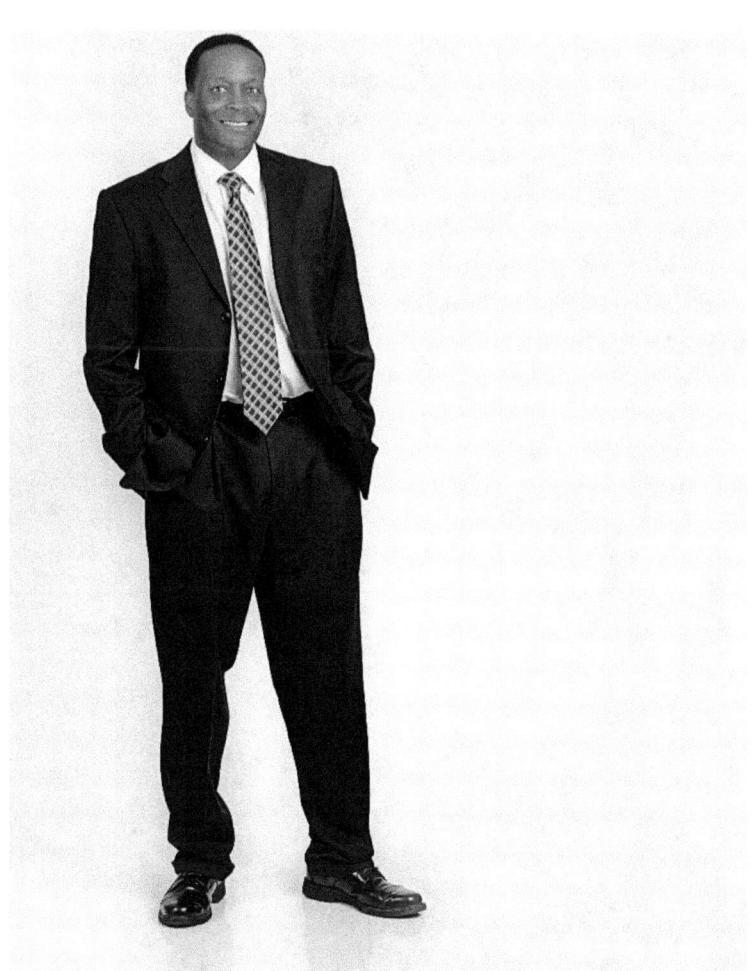

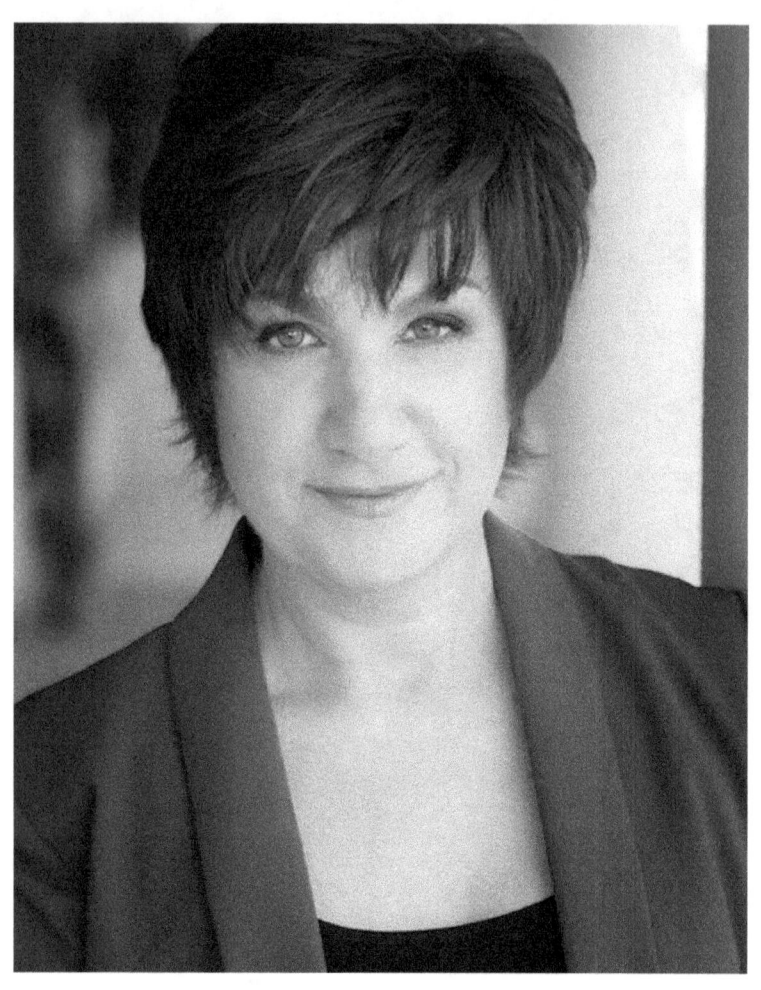

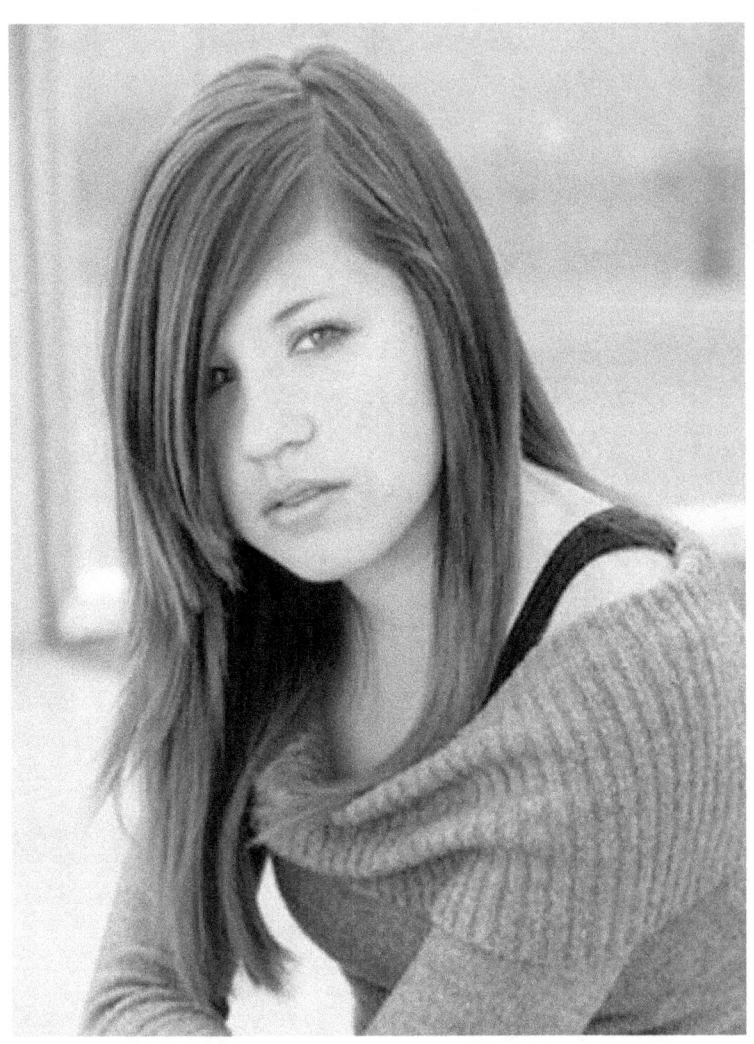

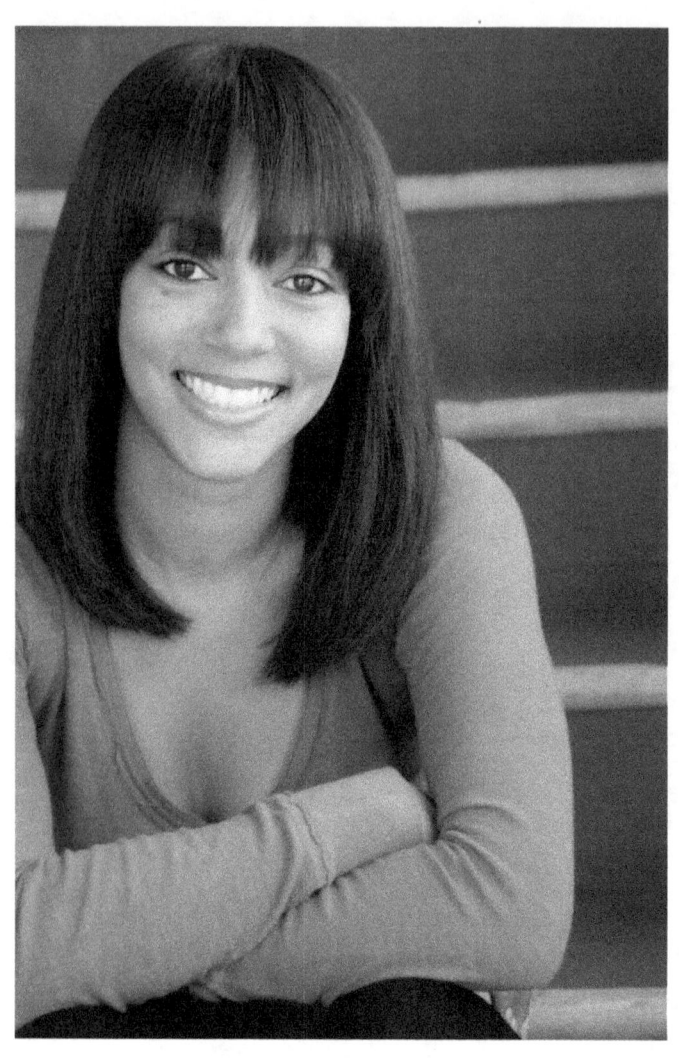

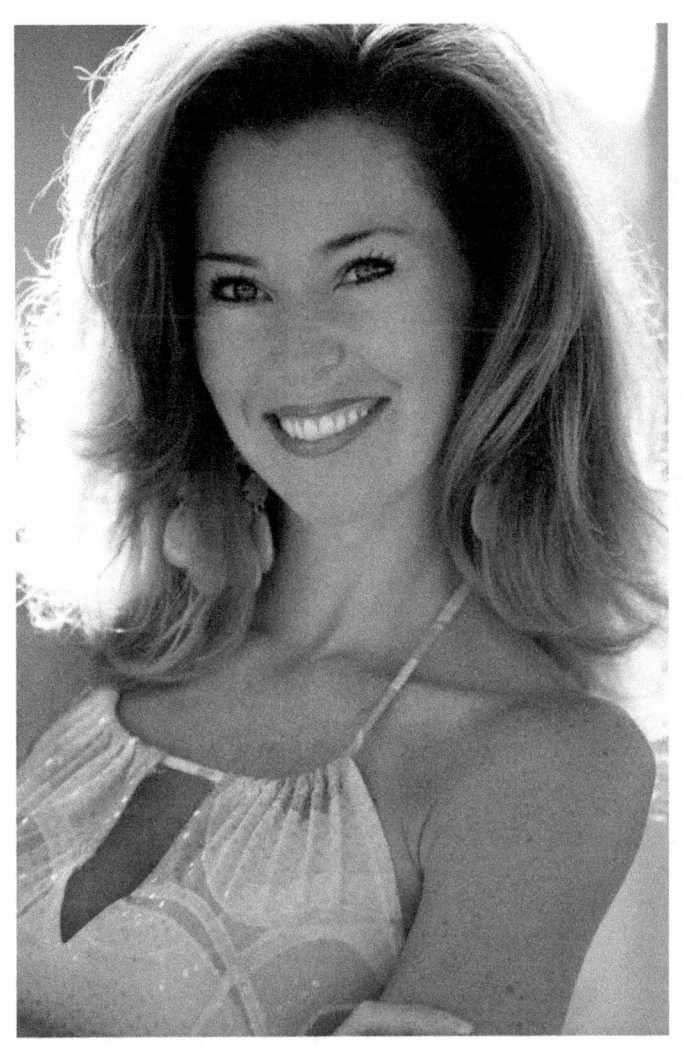

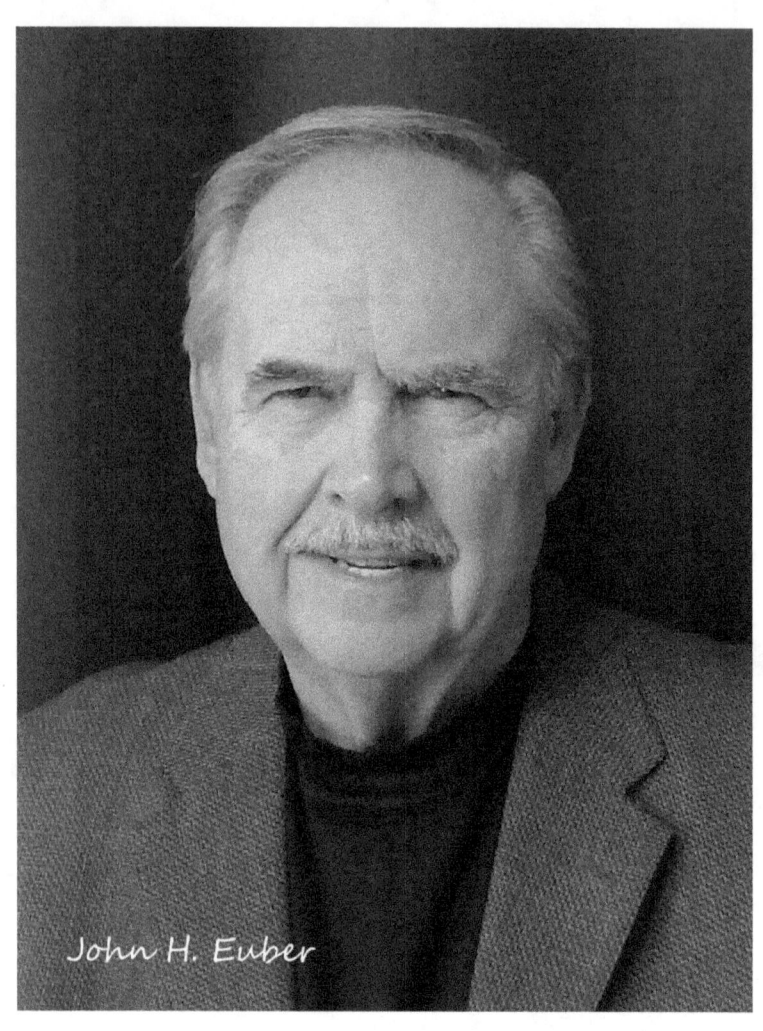

John H. Euber

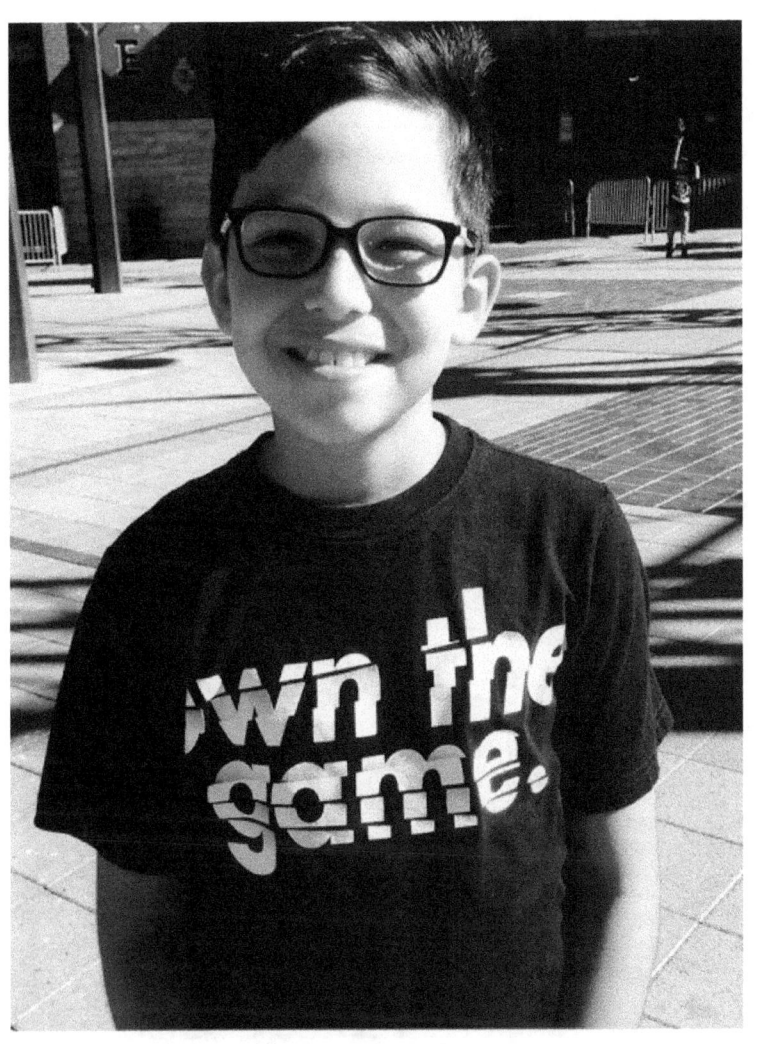

147

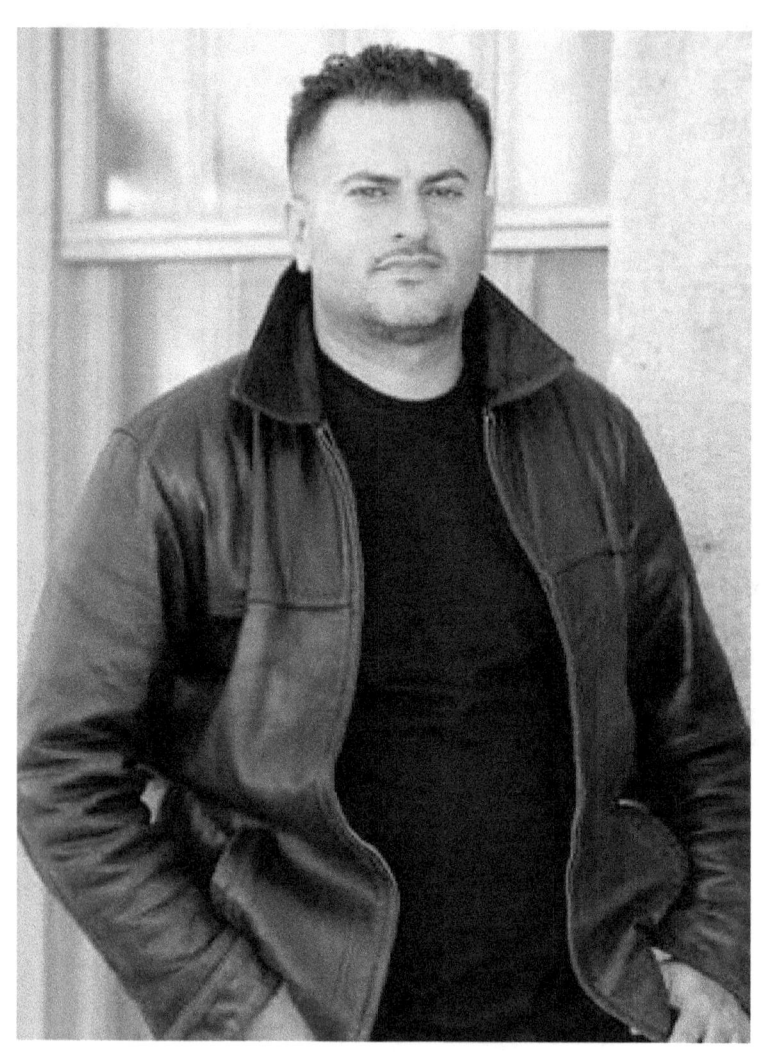

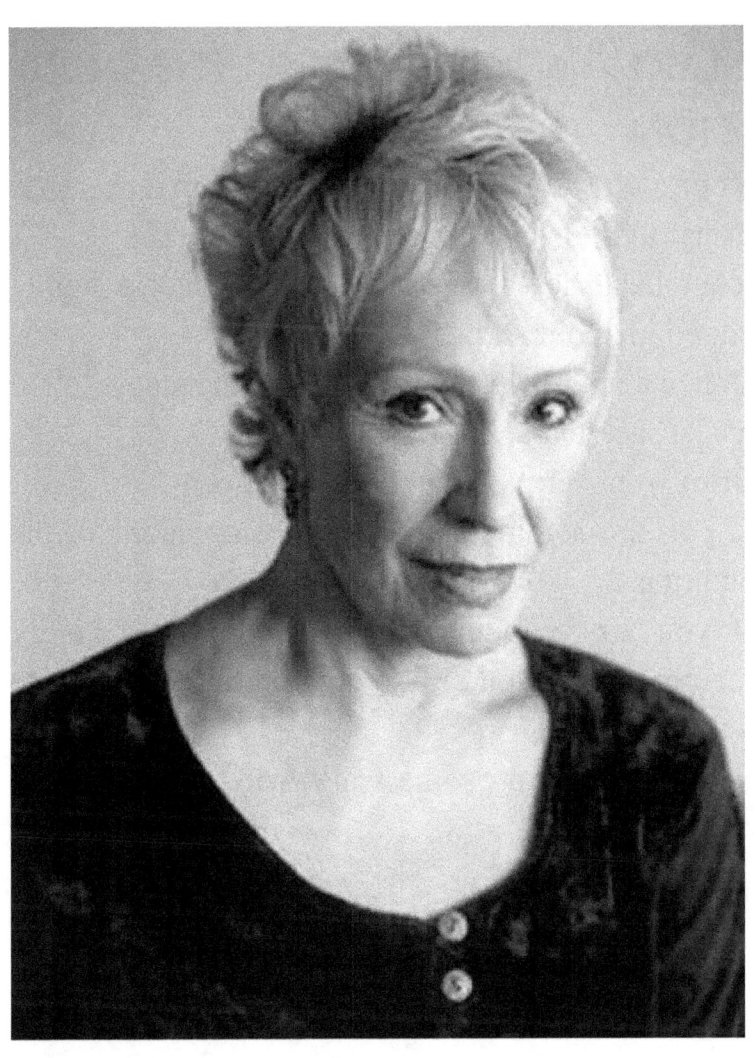

SUMMARY: WHAT TO BRING TO YOUR AUDITION

1. Your tools are your calling card and are required at every audition.
2. Your headshot must be current and not a highly edited glamour shot.
3. Create a simple resume for clients and staple to the back (back to back) of your headshot.
4. Bring your script, a highlighter and pen.
5. If you are a minor, bring only one parent to the audition.
6. If you are an adult, do not bring other family members with you unless you are not comfortable with the location.
7. Feel free to bring some water and a snack to the audition.

CHAPTER 13

ARRIVING AT THE AUDITION

These basic guidelines for arriving and checking in at the audition are common sense, but still need to be emphasized to ensure things go smoothly for the casting director.

SHOW UP FOR YOUR AUDITION

This is a "no brainer." If you commit to an audition appointment, made by your agent, then please show up. Emergencies happen, and exceptions are made, if it is an actual emergency. Notify the casting director's office or your agent. An agent will assume you showed up if they do not hear from you and will hope that you book the job. Also, you may have taken a spot from someone else who could have been there.

At a recent audition, eight actors did not show up. That hurts both the casting process and the agent's pocketbook, as the agent makes money *only* when talent book a job. "No-show" talent may not get a second chance with agents and the casting director will think twice about selecting them again. I try to notify the agents of the no-shows, so they are aware of their talents actions.

ARRIVING LATE OR EARLY

Please notify us, or your agent, if you are going to be late. We will make an exception, if it is only a few minutes (up to half an hour). Do not arrive two hours late. When actors show up to their audition several hours late, the audition may be over. By that time, I have packed up the equipment, closed the casting and am usually converting and uploading clips. I cannot stop what I am doing to put an actor on tape so don't bother showing up.

Arriving fifteen minutes early is preferred unless it is a cold read then show up thirty minutes early to get the script. Many *new* people will show up an hour early! There may be limited seating or other reasons why this is an inconvenience for the staff. If you find yourself early, try going for a walk around the block to kill some time and this will also help calm the nerves. Trust me you will make yourself more nervous sitting there and being so early.

KNOW THE AUDITION LOCATION

This seems like a simple thing, especially if the actor has auditioned before with the casting director. Many casting directors rent space and move around from time to time, but I decided to buy a stupid business condo that I could no longer afford after the "planned" housing market crash in 2008. After ditching my condo, I used three different locations to hold auditions. Inevitably, I have at least one or two actors instinctively go to my old facility (which is now a law firm...go figure, I think the lawyers planned this!). By the time they realized they were at the wrong place, it was too late, or they gave up. It is the actor's responsibility to know where to go! Verify the address and be sure to read your e-mail in its entirety.

CHECKING IN

When you are ready to check in with the casting director's staff, be friendly to everyone you meet (including the person checking you in whom may even be the casting director taking a break from the crazy audition). Don't say, "my headshot is in the car, do you need one?" Always assume we will need a headshot and resume, and bring it with you, already stapled. Again, and again, an actor hands me a headshot and then, pulls out a resume separately. I must then situate it and staple it for him, and this gets old after about the second one.

SIGNING IN

So, you showed up ready to audition and you walk in the casting director's office. Do you think it is a good idea to let someone know you are there or should you silently just sit in the waiting room and not say a word? I can't tell you how many times I have walked out to the waiting room only to see an actor sitting in a seat for hours and hours with a "what about me" look on his face only to realize his name is not on the sign in form. So much of this stuff is just plain common sense but people seem to be lacking it now due to all the toxins in our food and air and water!

AUDITION PAPERWORK

There is normally a casting form to fill out where we obtain your contact information, agent information (if you have one), personal stats and so on. In addition, there will be a sign-in sheet where you will list your name, agent name (if you have one) and phone number. If it is a SAG casting, you will need to fill in your arrival time and appointment time.

Side note here regarding a SAG casting: We must use special SAG sign-in form for the audition, so we can track how long the actor was there for the casting. If we run more than an hour long for any given actor, then the production company will get penalized and the actor will get compensated for his time (after one hour). Trust me it is not fun to get yelled out by a blow hard SAG president who thinks the world is going to end because a SAG audition ran late, or proper forms were not used. I could go on and on about SAG castings and SAG presidents, especially the one that used to be in place in Arizona, but my therapist told me to move on.

TIME CONFLICTS

If you have an appointment right after your audition, you must pick up your kids from school or you are on a lunch break from work, please notify staff upon check-in of your tight schedule. They will do their best to accommodate you and we understand that you are busy. All casting offices may not feel the same way, but it does not hurt to politely inform them of your situation. Many clients forget that actors have lives outside of *La-La land,* but I understand this as I can relate more to the actors because without them I would not have a paycheck.

On another note, it is important to allow for extra time during your audition. If, for some reason, you cannot stay, please notify the check-in person. Never be rude to the check-in person but do politely ask if they can tell you how much longer it may take. If you are rude, word will spread, and there may be a different mindset about you when you come into the audition room. Always expect to have to wait a while during the audition process and allow extra time for this.

Summary: Arriving at the Audition

1. Only commit to your audition if you are certain to attend.
2. Call the casting director's office or agent if you are unable to attend the audition.
3. Know the location of your audition before going.
4. Always bring your headshot and resume with you for check in.
5. Be sure to sign in at the audition, so you do not get overlooked.
6. Always be polite to the staff.
7. Allow yourself plenty of time at the audition; expect to have some wait time (which is normal).

CHAPTER 14

PLAYING THE WAITING GAME

While waiting to go into the audition room, use your time wisely. It is common for auditions to run late. Several things can throw the audition's timing off: unprepared actors are the most common factor because so much extra time is needed to explain things to them.

Here are the most common problem areas.

LAST CHANCE TO VERIFY THAT YOU HAVE THE SCRIPT

It is your responsibility to make sure you have received the script or storyboard for your audition. I can't stress this point enough. An actor's arriving unprepared is bothersome to the casting director and interrupts the casting process. Do not wait to walk into the audition room, only to say you did not get a script; please make sure you have gotten one before coming in! This happens so often, and I have a mini meltdown every time! Now is your last opportunity to clear this up. Some casting directors may not be lenient when this happens, and you may be sent home due to being unprepared.

Your agent may also be notified of the reason you mentioned for not having a script. Trust me, if you blame your agent, it will get back them!

In addition to having your script, know which role you are reading. I have had actors come in to read for parts that were not selected for them. They assumed a role was theirs and did not clear this up with their agents or the casting check-in person, beforehand. One might start to read the lines of the "heroine," when the role was the office worker, or one is reading the lines of the male role and is a female. When in doubt, verify your role before coming to the audition.

BEING NERVOUS

Telling you to not be nervous is like saying "Try not to breathe." A certain degree of nervousness is healthy. It gets your energy up. You must deal with your nerves without fixating on them. Try not to sit there thinking, *"I'm not nervous...I'm not nervous"* meanwhile your hearts beating so fast and you feel like you are going to lose your bowels and the runway train of nervousness is on the loose. A trick I use is to breathe in confidence and love (for thyself) and to breathe out "fear". You may find you feel a little euphoric and not as afraid. Force your mind to move away from your nervousness, concentrate on your script and how you can bring yourself to the words. Think of us in our underwear! Anything to make you realize we are all just human like you! Do not be intimidated by us in the back room because you are wasting your time. We are a mix of society just like you.

Don't beat yourself up by thinking you are not right for the role. You may see people there that look nothing like you. If you have been called in for the audition, assume you are right for the role.

NOISE LEVEL WHILE WAITING

Unacceptably high noise level is an ongoing problem at all auditions. Actors who are waiting are excited to see their fellow actors and, if you are in a smaller market, they all know each other. Kind of like the island of Maui! Keep focused and quiet while waiting. You are not there to make friends but to get a job. This is also distracting to us in the audition room. A funny thing happened during my Go Daddy auditions regarding this. My ex-husband, who normally cannot stand being at the office during auditions, was very excited to be at work for some reason during my Go Daddy auditions. Okay it was due to the hot chicks coming in, don't kid yourself. He was there with bells on and set himself up in the office that could look out at the models and pretty females lining up waiting to go into the audition room. He pretended to be "working" and instead was watching and listening to the models chatting it up as many of them knew each other from past jobs. It started sounding like a gaggle of geese as the volume increased and his enthusiasm quickly became deflated as the conversations were mainly about kids and their insecurities. Not sure what he was expecting but he finally gave up and went home after a couple of hours. LOL!

CELL PHONES

Turn off your phone or put it on silent! Enough said, here.

GUM CHEWING

Never chew gum during an audition. Please dispose of it before entering the audition room.

RESTROOM USE

Always use the restroom before your audition.

SUMMARY: PLAYING THE WAITING GAME

1. Always verify that you have your script and you know which your role is *before* going into the audition room.
2. Being nervous is healthy but do not fixate on your nerves.
3. Keep the noise level down and stay focused while waiting to audition.
4. Turn your cell phone off.
5. Never chew gum.
6. Be sure to use the restroom, especially if a minor.

CHAPTER 15

MAKING YOUR GRAND ENTRANCE

Your name has been called and it is now time to enter the room. Keep in mind that you are being assessed from the moment you enter. Directors and casting directors can read your body language as soon as you step into the room, so it is important to exude confidence right from the start!

Directions you will hear during the audition:

"Take your mark"-*Stand on the mark that has been put on the floor for you. Most likely just a piece of tape!*

"Roll camera"-*Instruction for the camera operator to begin recording.*

"Slate your name"-*Tell us your name on camera (always do this with a smile).*

"Give me a profile"-*Turn your entire body to the right, and then left. Do not just turn your head!*

"Action!"-*Your cue to begin your lines or action.*

"Cut!"-*Audition is over, and camera is stopped.*

AUDITION ROOM SETUP

A typical audition room has a table and chairs on one side and an open space (where the actor will stand) on the opposite side. Usually, there will be a solid background behind the actor and a studio light or lights directed at the actor. The casting director sits behind a table facing the actor(s) and the camera operator is in the center of the room, opposite and facing the actor as well. In most of auditions, I have done, the camera is on a tripod and not hand-held.

There is usually a table or chair where you can leave your purse, keys, cell phone, ego, nerves or briefcase, when you enter the room. If not, put them on the floor, out of sight of the camera lens.

WALKING INTO THE AUDITION ROOM

Unlike at a job interview, when you enter the audition room, it is preferable that you *do not* extend your hand to shake ours, because directors and casting directors do not want to risk catching a cold or another disease that actors carry such as nervousness. Keep in mind, you are just one person, but sometimes, up to 150 people are seen in one day! A friendly "hello" will suffice, then walk to your mark and be ready to receive your direction. I have had actors come in and want to give me a big loveable hug when I have never met them as they feel it will win some brownie points. I am all for hugging and in Hawaii it is very common, but this is not the place to do this.

POSITIVE ENERGY

Casting directors are rooting for you to do a good job. We are on your side! Everyone prefers actors who exude happy energy and have a sparkle in their eye from the moment they walk in. Actors who appear easy to work with and have a professional demeanor will do well. Be friendly but genuine, we can tell if it is just a phony act.

Never walk in the room and say, "This is my first audition" or "I am new at this." Even though it may be true, casting directors and *especially clients!* do not like hearing this, so, it is never a good way to start off your audition. Be positive, be confident and tell yourself you *can* do this!

Recently two actors were booked for a local cable commercial by the client, who did not audition them first, but selected them off their photos. When the actors (who were somewhat new to the industry) arrived, they both kept apologizing for being new and were so *un*confident, that a lot of stress was put on the director and, in turn, the client was very upset. The actors expected to do a bad job before even giving it a try! So, once again, never apologize. Keep your energy high and be as confident as you can possibly be! If they had only done this, the client may have never known they were new. Although the director was able to get some usable footage, it was a challenge for everyone involved.

DIRECTION FROM THE CASTING DIRECTOR

After entering and taking your mark, you are ready to listen to direction, so, I will give a quick explanation of how to proceed. I usually ask the actor to do a simple name slate (more on this in next paragraph) and then I explain where to stand and sometimes even where to look (or have your "eye line"), during the scene. If the script calls for more than one person, I will let you know who is going to be reading with you. It may be me (from off camera) or another actor, standing by your side.

A word of caution, the direction you are given may go completely against how you rehearsed the scene. You will be thrown off guard and immediately go into a panic. I literally have had actors tell me "that is not how I rehearsed it" and were determined to only do it their way. The key here is to always remain flexible and *like* how you rehearsed it but do not fall in love with it. Walk in the audition room with an open mind and listen to the direction given and take a moment to let it sink in. Realize that we may have a better idea of how the client wants' it played out.

If you have any questions about the script, now is the time to ask for clarification. Please *do not* ask me "What is my motivation?" I chuckle every time I am asked this! *One of my favorite Alfred Hitchcock quotes is: "When an actor comes to me and wants to discuss his character, I say, 'It's in the script.' If he says, 'But what's my motivation? I say, 'Your salary."* I did a belly laugh when I read this! Sorry to say, most casting directors do not intellectualize the roles. What we want is what you personally can give us. There are many layers to acting like an onion, but I truly consider myself only on the outer layer and you can explore your own onion in your acting class.

SLATING YOUR NAME

Every audition starts with you, doing a simple slate. This is where you say your first and last name, and agent's name (if you have one), on camera. It is as simple as saying, "Hi, my name is Joey Roberts and I am with Zoolander Agency." Do not worry if you do not have an agent, just say you are unrepresented. If you are asked to say *only* your first and last name, then make sure to say *only* this! Do not say your agent's name...period; you must *listen* and *hear* the direction given! We know who your agent is because you put it on your paperwork! Always enunciate your name clearly. Give a smile after your slate and hold it for a pause. You may need to turn and give us a profile, so turn your *entire* body to the right and then left, slowly. Do not turn just you're your head from side to side quickly as you will look like a fool. Always remember to smile during your slate and profile. When clients are viewing your audition, if you show a lack of *something* (fill in the blank depending on the client) in your slate, your audition may be passed up quickly or, worse, they may not even watch it!

SCRIPTS

It is best to hold on to your script during your read, unless directed otherwise. Many times, the actor feels he has it memorized but, time and time again, will make mistakes, due to nerves. Many times, I have asked a new talent if they need their script and they proudly say "no" only to then see them standing there with a blank look and confusion as they try to recall their lines. I then ask them again if they need their script and they again (less proudly) say "no" and then stand there once again with that same expression. I finally must tell them firmly "Please pick up your script!"

Try not to make too much noise with the script as the camera will pick up the sound and it will be distracting and remember to *NOT* hold it up high to where it covers your face. I have actors hold the script in front of their face time and time again and I guess they think it is about how their script looks on camera rather than their face.

GLASSES

If you wear glasses, ask us if we would like them on or off. If you need them to see your script, then wear them for your audition. We do not want to see you squinting during your read. Hopefully you have memorized your lines and do not need your glasses! If you get booked for the job you will have time to memorize your lines. In addition, the project is filmed in blocks and not all at once.

ACTIONS/PROPS

If you are auditioning for say an automobile commercial. Most likely you are sitting in a chair in an audition room, working with thin air. Keep your actions simple. You do not have to go through all the physical motions you normally would while sitting in a car. Less is more in this case. If your character is talking on the phone, you do not have to pantomime holding a phone. Just act natural and have the conversation and remember to listen and react as well. On a side note; my clients tend to feel their way is the right way and they are never the same when it comes to props. Some want you to hold or work with the prop, like a telephone and others have a cow if you dare want to hold your hand near your head as if talking on a telephone. Their righteous attitude towards actors is a little annoying but I must remember that they are just humans with lots of flaws themselves.

You may have to audition for a food or beverage ad and you may be given a stale food item or warm beverage to eat or drink. The actual eating or drinking of this item will be judged.

A good acting coach can help you develop natural skills when doing certain actions and working with props.

TALKING DURING THE AUDITION

Keep your talking to a minimum and only speak if you have a question or need the direction again. Most problems with excessive talking occur during group auditions. At a recent commercial audition, I brought the actors in 5 at a time. I went down the line of actors, with the camera on each, and gave direction during a non-speaking bit. They were asked to improvise facial expressions, directly to camera. A female in the line kept laughing out loud and commenting on the other actor's performances. Yes, they were all very funny, but I finally had to tell her to please be quiet, so we could continue. Please do not comment or give your opinion during another actor's read.

AUDITION TIMEFRAME

For a commercial audition, you have about five to ten minutes, total, so you must make every moment count. A lot of new actors are surprised to see how very little time they get in the audition room. *Never* rush through your audition or speed up your talking unless directed otherwise. During the audition, we want to (*and* like to) see more. Once you hear the word "action" take a pause (which is known as a *beat*) to collect yourself and then get in the scene. You do not win an award for the fastest start but on the other hand try to not take more than a few seconds to start.

If you only have one line to deliver such as "Special delivery for Mr. Jones", do not drag out the line to say "speeeccciiaallll deeeelivvverrryyy foooorrrr Misssterrr Joooonnneesss" as if reading Shakespeare. A simple delivery is key.

ARROGANCE

Leave your ego at home, unless you are Kid Rock and can back it up. Egos are a big turn-off. Being confident is important, but being arrogant is another thing, entirely. Once, an experienced actor showed up for a commercial audition where there were no lines, just reactions to the action. He smirked and rolled his eyes during his audition, as if it were a big joke. His body language screamed, "I am too good for this." That was not the reaction required, so the joke was on him because he was never invited back for another audition.

Regarding commercial auditions keep in mind commercials are *silly!* So, get over it and don't be afraid to be goofy. Always have a positive and friendly attitude and never take yourself too seriously.

Summary: Making your Grand Entrance

1. When entering, do not shake hands.
2. Exude happy, positive energy, when entering the room.
3. Listen to the casting director, hear the direction and follow it.
4. Learn to "slate" your name with a smile and enthusiasm.
5. Keep your talking to a minimum, during the audition.
6. Do not be afraid to ask questions, if you need more clarity.
7. Do your best, within your given timeframe, for the audition.
8. Leave your ego at home.

CHAPTER 16

KEEPING YOUR NERVES AND BODY IN CHECK

When you are nervous, everyone gets nervous. Sometimes, the energy of the nervous actor is so thick; it can almost be cut with a knife. New actors have nervous habits that are obvious and distract from their performance, such as: sweating profusely, swaying back and forth, pulling or tugging on their clothes, eyes darting from one side of the room to the other, quivering mouths, ending the audition too soon, not following direction or laughing inappropriately. Most do not even realize they are doing these things.

It is very important to be aware of your body, so that you can correct and overcome the problem areas, which are so distracting.

BODY FRAMING

When filming the audition, a couple of different takes are usually required. Within those takes, the camera operator may zoom in on you and crop the frame tight, so the client can see your facial expressions, or they may film the frame looser allowing your body to show and, so they can see certain actions. Keep in mind that these shots may be converted to smaller QuickTime clips and then uploaded online for our client to view. I like to inform the actor of the framing, so they are careful of their body movements. If you are making distracting body movements, it will look very awkward on your audition clip and the client will move on to the next actor. Feel free to ask the casting director how the framing will be as they may not provide this information.

SWAYING

It is common for inexperienced actors to sway from side to side during their audition. This looks funny especially if we are framing you tightly. To avoid this, practice planting both of your feet on the ground. We call this "grounding" in hippie terms. Take a second to really feel your feet touching the ground and the weight of your legs rooted to the center of the earth. Keep them planted there, and then proceed with your audition. It may feel awkward at first, but it will make you more aware of how much you were swaying before. You will eventually be able to work naturally within the small space allowed during an audition.

A good audition read usually comes from an actor that is using his thoughts which are projecting through his eyes more than his body language. Basically, acting from the head up. This is called a "believable" read because he is thinking, listening and reacting and we can see this, and he draws us in.

BUSY HANDS

Pay attention to your hand movements. Do not tug on your clothes or play with your hair or other distracting gestures. In normal conversation, we gesture all the time, without even thinking about it. Rely on your *gut instincts* as to where these gestures come in. You will eventually be able to have your hands by your sides naturally or gesture naturally, without being distracting.

WHERE TO LOOK

This is important! When you are doing an audition, lack of focal point will make you look very unsure of yourself. Most likely you will be told where to have your "eye line". If not...please ask! Keep in mind the reference points you are given are not for you *stare* at but do your best to "look" at them naturally. This may be the microphone that is on top of the camera or a picture on the wall or the casting director. If you are having a dialogue with someone and are supposed to be looking at him, do not switch your focal point mid-dialogue to include us. We are there to watch and observe only so pretend we are not even there.

CHEAT IT TO THE CAMERA

The term "cheat it to camera" is very common among auditions. Think about a time when you were involved in a conversation; normally you are facing the other person. On camera, if you did this, we would only be able to see your profile and it can make for a very boring audition. In auditions with another actor, rather than turn to the side to face them, face your body more towards camera and cheat your face to camera as well. This allows us to see your facial expressions while you are reacting to the other actor. Take an on-camera audition class to understand this better.

SUMMARY: KEEPING YOUR NERVES AND BODY IN CHECK

1. Be aware of distracting body movements, during your audition.
2. Rather than sway back and forth while doing your audition, plant both of your feet firmly on the ground.
3. Pay attention to your hand movements, but also incorporate natural gestures.
4. Ask the casting director where your focal point should be.
5. Always "cheat" your face and body to camera, unless told otherwise.

CHAPTER 17

YOUR

PERFORMANCE

You are now ready to show us your performance. Remember to breathe during your audition and do not rush through your lines. Even though you may have rehearsed your script a hundred times, your lines need to be delivered as if for the "very first time". *(meaning: think of going to the movie and watching the actors. The actor says the most amazing things and really draws you in. You have no idea the actor's dialogue and what is coming up next, so those lines are heard for the "very first time" by you).* Clients want to be captured by words they wrote and want you to draw them in. Commercial auditions are comical because the clients think they are shooting a blockbuster feature film and a lot of importance is placed on the delivery of the words. Your words must sound natural and flow smoothly through the different emotional changes. When we ask, "are you ready?" you are then in command so take command!

DOING YOUR LINES

If you have not memorized the material, do not fake it. Rather, hold your script down low and use it for a reference. Do not shuffle the paper around. Try to keep it still or the microphone will pick up the sound. *Never* add your own dialogue to the script, unless you have been told to improvise by the casting director. The client likes the lines just the way they were written and wants to hear them during the reading.

REACTING TO THE CAMERA

If we direct you to look in the camera we need to see the energy in your eyes. The audition space is very unforgiving, and you are usually being filmed in a tight frame. Relate to the camera as if it were the person you are doing the scene with. Rather than looking *at* the camera, look *through* it. Have strong visuals in your mind that allow you to see what or whom you are supposed to be looking at and talking to. Put yourself in the room with that person and visualize having a dialogue. Forget about everyone else in the room and make us believe you are there. Don't internalize how silly you look or start the negative chatter in your mind. Focus and stay in the moment.

AUDITIONING WITH OTHER ACTORS

It is important that you are friendly and responsive to the other actors in the room with you. Most likely they are nervous too! Say hello to them when you enter the room but do not engage them in a full-on conversation about life. You have limited time in the audition room.

Get used to standing very close to the other actor, for framing purposes. Otherwise, you appear awkward, as if you cannot relate to each other. On a monitor, it looks completely normal for you to be close enough to touch the other actor with your elbow. Pay attention to your body language. The scene may call for you to have an intimate conversation. Turn your body a little inward towards him. Do not turn your body or face completely sideways and once again, always "cheat it to camera." Unless directed otherwise we need to see your faces.

React to what the other actor is saying. One can always tell when the actor is only thinking of his next line. This kind of performance will never get you the job. Acting is reacting, so, when you watch TV or go to the movies, pay attention to the actors who are not talking. They are listening and reacting naturally. You must do this, as well, or you will not get called back...ever.

If you are with an actor that makes mistakes, keep on going to show us you are not the one with the problem. There have been a few times where I had to dismiss the bad actor to enable the decent actor to do the read without them. If an actor's performance is poor, we do not include them in our casting link.

MAKING A MISTAKE

If you make a mistake during your audition, the best thing to do is to continue. If it is at the beginning, you may start again but do not beat yourself up (internally). Do not fixate on the mistake you just made. We do not care if you make a mistake. Keep your humor. You will most likely get a second chance, but your ability to recover is even more important than delivering perfect lines. Even experienced actors make mistakes when auditioning, so, do not stop the audition. Just keep going!

If you continue to make mistakes, again and again, and again, you most likely will not get the job, because it shows that you will be unable to do what is asked of you, on set. Don't worry about making excuses, no matter how justified, excuses sound like excuses.

STAYING IN THE SCENE

Inexperienced actors will do a line and then quickly look up at me, hoping for a reaction or comment. They have a hard time letting it flow and staying in the scene, or they will deliver their lines too quickly and then look up at the end, hoping for a reaction. Never do this! Stay in the scene until you hear "cut!" There may be an important reaction needed from you, *after* the lines are delivered, but you are ending it too soon, due to nerves.

OVERACTING/UNDER ACTING

New actors tend to either make bland boring choices or overact, rather than keeping it simple and real. They tend to talk too fast, talk to loud or soft and exaggerate facial expressions. Making good natural choices is key so avoid making bizarre choices. The clients want you to be believable. I hear this again and again during callbacks. They will say things like, "she was not real" or "I did not buy her" or "he was not believable" or "he was too over the top." Acting for film and TV is very different from acting for theatre. Remember, auditions must be very conversational in nature, but we do need to know that you have a pulse. Let us see your real personality!

ADDITIONAL REQUESTS

Many times, after an actor does his read I notice they may be good for another role so I hand them different sides to perform. If you can help it do not cold read right, then and there. Ask if you can take some time outside of the room to prepare these new lines that were just handed to you. I normally do not have a problem with this and it reminds me that you are human and need a little time.

NEGATIVE COMMENTS

Do not make negative comments about yourself on camera. I have seen smiling actors whose face immediately changes to a grimace after their performance and they say things like "darn" or "I blew it" or "ugghhh". This is the last thing anyone watching those clips will see...your contorted face after you say your lines.

CUT / THANK YOU

When we say the word "cut" that is the queue for the camera operator to stop rolling camera and for you to stop performing. Do not stop until we say this word. Stay in the moment as long as possible. Once we say, "thank you" you are done and free to leave.

LEAVING

After completing your audition, a simple farewell will do and, once again, do not shake our hands, hug us and never apologize for your performance.

FEEDBACK

Actors love to ask for my feedback after they audition, I normally do not give this because during their audition I directed them to switch things up if I did not like what I was seeing. Keep in mind that the selection process comes down to the client and their visions and I rarely have anything to do with it. Do your best and then move on. The only time you may get feedback is when you did something wrong (like coming in unprepared).

GIVING THANKS

If your agent set up the audition for you, thank them! Call or e-mail to let them know how the audition went. They will feel appreciated by you and remember you as a polite and grateful actor.

SUMMARY: YOUR PERFORMANCE

1. If your lines are not memorized, do not fake it or improvise.
2. Use your script and hold it down low, if necessary.
3. Forget about everyone else in the room and visualize the person or persons you are talking to. Make us believe you are there.
4. If working with another actor, know the framing so you can adjust your position appropriately. Do not be afraid to stand very close.
5. Always react to what others are saying as well...*acting is reacting.*
6. Do not look up, hoping to get a reaction from us or end it too early.
7. Stay in the scene until you hear "cut," which lets you know the audition or take is over.
8. Do not over act...keep it natural.
9. A simple "thank you" is enough, upon leaving; do not apologize for your performance.
10. You may not get any feedback. If you did your best, move on and we will be in touch if you are called back.

CHAPTER 18

DISH ON CASTING DIRECTORS

Of all the egos in this industry, some of the biggest you will encounter may belong to the casting director. Casting directors have very different approaches to actors and auditions. They can create a very positive experience or a horrible one (where you vow never to audition again!). If you have done your homework, you have nothing to worry about. If, on the other hand, you have not done your homework and are unprepared, you may be in for a very rude awakening.

CONSTRUCTIVE CRITICISM

It is important to learn from and heed any advice you receive from the casting director during the audition. If they suggest ways to improve your read, use them. Be a good listener! If I have time, I may point out things to inexperienced talent during their audition. I may even give them a few more chances on camera to improve their audition. Many times, though, we do not have time to do this, so we always prefer the actor to train on his own time.

RUDE CASTING DIRECTORS

I have already mentioned never being rude to the staff or casting director; I also need to mention the casting director's being rude to you. I am not speaking about rejection or constructive criticism, which is part of the industry, but just plain rudeness. Some casting directors can be condescending or have inflated egos. I have heard horror stories and witnessed this behavior, in person. I had the experience of handling extras casting for a large studio feature film and the casting coordinator from Los Angeles made for a very unpleasant experience. She was rude to the actors auditioning for some very key roles and several of them left before auditioning. Having a bad attitude and treating actors, who are there to audition, poorly, just makes zero sense to me.

Never take it personally, remain professional always and, later, you can choose whether to return to that casting director. You may eventually decide that this industry is not for you because you are a sensitive soul and that is perfectly okay. It is not for everyone!

SUMMARY: DISH ON CASTING DIRECTORS

1. Some of the biggest egos belong to casting directors.
2. Heed their advice and learn from their constructive criticism.
3. Do not take it personally, if they are rude.
4. If you have done your homework and given a good performance, you have nothing to worry about.
5. If you had a bad experience at a casting call, you can choose whether to audition with that casting director in the future.

CHAPTER 19

CALLBACK AUDITION

When the initial round of casting is over, it is time to bring in the actual decision makers for what is known as a "callback" audition. If the actor did his homework and the casting director did her job then there will be several qualified actors to choose from, for each given role.

CALLBACK

The callback audition gives the director or ad agency another chance to see your performance, but in person, now. It also allows them to see the chemistry between two or more actors. The callback audition normally includes the director, producer, ad agency creative's and, many times, the actual client or company representative.

It can be quite intimidating to now have about ten people staring at you from the other side of the table. Especially when they look like the most stressed out people you could ever meet in your whole life! The stress level of the director, producer, studio heads, ad agency and creative's can be intense, and they may not be overly friendly. Never take this personal and it has nothing to do with you. Tell yourself you are the answer to their problems. Think it and feel it and show it. They will be thankful they called you back for a second look. Be proud you made it this far.

CALLBACK PROTOCOLS

Do your performance just like the first time (unless instructed otherwise) and try to wear the same clothes but it is not imperative especially if they have stains on them now. Do not ask who everyone is, as it is a waste of time. Time, you can use to show off your acting skills. Remember; do not shake their hands as they do not need any more frazzled nerves. Just enter the room, quietly take your mark and wait for your queue to begin. Once again, after the "action" request is given...you are in command. Take command!

LISTENING TO THE DIRECTOR

Callbacks are my favorite part of the auditions because I know we are close to having a successful casting. It is very exciting to see directors in action, working with talent. I have learned so much by watching the callbacks and it has helped me tremendously with my casting sessions. Enjoy this process and learn from it, too!

Clients criticize, comment and argue over actors during callback auditions. They are like "armchair quarterbacks" but keep in mind most of them could not do what you are doing!

In most callbacks, the actual director will give the direction to the actors coming in rather than the casting director. It may be very different from what was done in the initial audition. You may have done a stellar performance and even better than I could have directed but you may still receive direction to do it a different way. This is just to see your flexibility. Keep an open mind and positive attitude always.

If the director seems upset, do not let it bother you. I have witnessed a few directors at callback in such bad moods. They are under so much stress to please their clients. The negative energy can be felt by all. Keep *your* energy and confidence up and brush off any negative energy you may feel upon walking in the door. Sometimes, the director will remain neutral, which is a sign of professionalism but can be somewhat frustrating for the actor. I have also seen directors act so happy and excited about an actor's performance that it made the actor feel he had won the role; just to learn later that he was not selected. The biggest rule is: be flexible and don't jump to any conclusions!

The director may also throw some improvised scenarios at you to see how quick you think on your feet.

He might also want to see if you can add something to the character. In one film audition, the director made each actor do their lines like their favorite relative. It made for a very comical audition. Don't be afraid to be silly! While some directors work fast and have the actor perform only one time before moving on to the next actor, other directors have you do it again and again and again and again and again and again and again and again and again and again and again. Keep in mind; this is the first time the director has seen the script with actual actors reading the lines. It helps him, as well, to prepare for the upcoming shoot.

EXITING AFTER YOUR CALLBACK

Stay in the scene and on your mark until you hear the words "cut" or "thank you." That means your audition is over and you can leave. A simple word of thanks from you is all that is needed. Do not ask when you will hear back and never ask if you got the part! Trust me, if you are chosen, we know how to get a hold of you.

One word of caution; after you leave the room, do not rush to your car; stay in the vicinity for a few minutes. Many times, the director decides, after you have left, to have you perform with another actor or for a different role. I must chase down the actor and oftentimes the actor has *left the building* like Elvis and lost a chance to impress the director even more.

SUMMARY: CALLBACK AUDITION

1. The callback audition allows the actors to have a second chance at impressing the director.
2. The callback allows the director to also prepare for the upcoming commercial.
3. Keep your performance the same unless directed otherwise.
4. Be flexible at the callback and open to what is thrown your way from the director.
5. Listen and learn from your experience at the callback.
6. Do not rush to your car, just in case you are requested back by the director.

CHAPTER 20

SELECTION PROCESS

The audition process is now over, and it is time to select the actors! I am even happier now! There is still a lot of work that goes into the decision-making process. I as a casting director have very little to do with the actual selections.

ORGANIZING CHOICES

During callbacks, the creative's have been taking notes on the actors, to remind them of their performances. Immediately after the callback, the creative's and director gather their top picks and spread the headshots out on a big table. They begin by matching up their notes and the headshots with the characters and then screening out actors who are not right. In this process, although you may have done well, you might get replaced by someone whose look matched the character better or they felt would be easier to work with. I am usually asked to play back a certain actor's performance and then, we might go back and forth for a while, like this. By the time we wrap up callback, the top picks and alternate picks are ready to be presented to the client. I then upload the top choices online for their upcoming pre-production meeting. Sometimes, I upload second and third choices as well, and then I play the waiting game. I am extremely relieved now because I am usually exhausted after a busy audition round and I can now go play.

PRE-PRODUCTION MEETING

Usually within one to two days, the creative's hold a pre-production meeting with the clients and present the actor choices. It ultimately comes down to the client to give the final say on who they want for their project. The director has a big say, as well because he is the one who must work directly with the actor, in the actual shoot.

BOOKING THE ACTORS

After the final choices have been made, I can pass on the good news to the actors and or their agents. We place them on hold for the actual shoot dates and they wait for the details of the upcoming job. Rarely does an actor hear back from anyone if he is not selected; the more experienced ones have learned to move on within a couple of days. You can definitely move on if the actual shoot dates have passed!

Do not beat yourself up if you do not get booked. You may have done well but were too short or tall or young or old or your performance was not what they wanted. In many cases it is about "pairings". The best people are not always cast. Many clients do not even know what they are looking for until they see it.

SUMMARY: SELECTION PROCESS

1. After callback, the top picks are shown to the client at a pre-production meeting and final selections are made.
2. The director has a big influence on the selection of actors.
3. Casting directors are rarely involved in the final selections.
4. If you have not heard anything and it has been several days, assume you did not get the role.
5. Do not beat yourself up if you were not booked.

CHAPTER 21

TO WRAP IT ALL UP

I only wish there was a guide for me starting out as a casting director. My inadequacies showed a lot at first, but I worked really hard to learn the ropes but more than that I created my own way of casting. I "made it my own dawg", as Randy from American Idol used to say. *(Remember I mentioned that film, TV and commercials have a huge influence on pop culture?)*.

Will you be perfect? Not in the least. Will you still make mistakes? *Absolutely!* Hopefully, the mistakes you make will not hurt your chances of getting booked.

Now I am finishing up with a couple of reminder checklists for you, in the hopes that what you read really sinks in. They are titled "Common Mistakes" and "Words of Advice".

Get your auditions skills on Actors!

COMMON MISTAKES

1. You think you do not need to train.
2. You think you are right for every role.
3. You try to pass yourself off as much younger.
4. You exaggerate your skills and abilities.
5. You enter the audition room, saying you did not get the script.
6. You have not rehearsed the script.
7. You do not know which role you are reading.
8. You are late to your audition appointment.
9. You are rude to the casting director's staff, at the audition.
10. You are unavailable for the shoot dates, but come to the audition anyway.
11. You wear distracting clothes with busy patterns.
12. Your hair is in your face.
13. You are impatient during your audition.
14. You did not bring your headshot or resume.
15. You have overly re-touched or outdated headshots.
16. You do not have your resume stapled to your headshot.
17. You shake our hands, upon entering the room.
18. You talk excessively before or during the audition.
19. You chew gum.
20. You do not notify anyone, if you are unable to make your audition appointment.
21. You did not work on your script before the audition.

22. You do not follow directions.
23. You hold back or are too conservative during the audition.
24. You apologize or say it is your first audition.
25. You do a dialect without being asked.
26. You add your own lines to the script.
27. You make bland, boring choices.
28. You over-act the lines and exaggerate facial expressions.
29. You hold the script in front of your face, during auditions.
30. You do not react to the other actor's lines, during the audition.
31. Your eye line is all over the room.
32. You look up at the casting director after saying a line hoping for a reaction.
33. You end your audition too soon.
34. You ask if you got the job.

WORDS OF ADVICE

1. Be positive at all times.
2. Do your homework before every audition.
3. Ensure you receive the script and understand the role you are reading.
4. Be sure to get some training for your creative muscle.
5. Keep your headshot and resume current and have them on hand, in case of a last-minute audition.
6. Staple your headshot and resume together, back to back, prior to the audition.
7. Wear comfortable, non-busy clothes that flatter your physique.
8. Be friendly to the other actors in the audition room.
9. Keep focused while waiting to audition.
10. Arrive on time for your audition appointment and notify someone if you are running late.
11. Allow for extra time, in case the auditions are running behind schedule.
12. Do your best to rehearse your script and memorize your dialogue.
13. Hold onto your script during the audition if necessary. Keep it down low and not in front of your face.
14. Practice your slate and be sure to give us a friendly smile.

15. Bring your own personality forward with every audition.
16. Be as real as possible.
17. Be honest about your skills.
18. Be flexible and open to direction from the casting director and director.
19. Keep body movements simple.
20. If unsure where to focus your eye line, be sure to ask.
21. Ask for clarification, before you start your performance.
22. If you flub lines do not start over, just keep going.
23. Do not beat yourself up, if you do mess up; everyone makes mistakes!
24. Take your time during your performance. We like to see more!
25. Stay in character until we say, "cut" or "thank you."
26. Radiate friendliness and show us that you are cooperative.
27. Don't beat yourself up if you think you did not do a good job.
28. Learn from your mistakes and always try to improve your performance.

CHAPTER 22

NOW GET GOING!

You have now come to the end and hopefully you have learned a few things along the way. I encourage you to use these tools at your next audition. Try to attend as many auditions as possible. Do not sit around and wait for the phone to ring. There are always resources for auditions in your area for student films, commercials, community theatre, independent films, cable TV and so much more.

Be sure to take a class or two, or ongoing series of classes, to better learn the audition process and acting in general. This will also help in networking and finding additional resources for auditions. Find like-minded actors with whom you can practice your craft. Stay positive and enjoy the process. Give it your best but remember your best may not be "their best" so never take it personal!

Sincerely,
Patrice Romero

CHAPTER 23

FILM COMMISSIONS

Here is a list of film commissions throughout the globe! I encourage you to contact one near you and inquire as to who does casting in your area. They may also provide you with a list of talent/modeling agents to reach out to and/or projects currently casting.

Abu Dhabi Film Commission
P.O. Box 77809
2454 Abu Dhabi
United Arab Emirates
+971-24012454
Algarve Film Commission
Rua 1 de Maio, 15-1
8000-411 Faro
Portugal
+351-289098208
Amsterdam Film Commission
Amstel 1
1011 NP Amsterdam
Netherlands
+31-651301197
Antwerp City Film Office
Francis Wellesplein 1
2018 Antwerp
Belgium

+32-33383147
Berlin Brandenburg Film Commission
c/o Medienboard Berlin-Brandenburg Gmbh
August-Bebel- Str. 26-53
D-14482 Potsdam-Babelsberg
Germany
+49-3317438730
Bermuda Tourism Authority
22 Church Street
Hamilton HM11
Bermuda
+1 (212) 916-3136
British Virgin Islands Film Commission
P. O. Box 134
Road Town
British Virgin Islands
Brugge City Film Office
Toerisme Brugge
Burg 12
8000 Brugge
Belgium
+32-50444646
Carinthia Film Commission
Kärnten Werbung GmbH
Völkermarkter Ring 21 - 23
AT-9020 Klagenfurt
Austria
+43-463300032
Cine Tirol Film Commission
Maria-Theresien-Str. 55
6020 Innsbruck
Austria
+43-5125320*ext.* 182

Colombian Film Commission
Calle 35 No. 5-89
Bogota, D.C.
Colombia
+57-2870103
Costa Rica Film Commission
Escazu, sobre Autopista Prospero Fernandez
Complejo Plaza Tempo, piso 3
1278-1007 San Jose
Costa Rica
+506-25054837
Czech Film Commission
State Cinematography Fund
Dukelskych Hrdinu 47
170 00 Praha 7
Czech Republic
+420-728132026
Dubai Film and TV Commission
Dubai Studio City, Commercial Building 1, Ground
Floor
53777 Dubai
United Arab Emirates
+971-43602022
FFF Film Commission Bavaria
Sonnenstrasse 21
80331 München
Germany
+49-8954460216
Film Commission Chile
Ahumada #11, 11th Floor
8320312 Santiago
Chile
+56-26189168

Film Commission Ecuador
Edificio la Licuadora
Ave Gran Colombia N11-165 y Gral Pedro Briceno
170412 Quito
Ecuador
+593-3999333
Film Commission Hamburg Schleswig-Holstein
Filmförderung HHSH GmbH
Friedensallee 14-16
22765 Hamburg
Germany
+49-40398370
Film Commission Norway
Norwegian Film Institute
P. Box 482 Sentrum
0105 Oslo
Norway
Film Commission Poland
ul. Chelmska 21, bud 4/56
00-724 Warsaw
Poland
+48 (69) 347 7607
Film Commission Region Stuttgart
Breitscheidstrasse 4
Bosch-Areal
70174 Stuttgart
Germany
+49-7112594430
Film France, The French Film Commission
9 rue du Chateau d'eau
75010 Paris
France
+33-153839898

Film In Iceland
Borgartun 35
IS-105 Reykjavik
Iceland
+354-5114000
Filming in Croatia
Nova Ves 18
10000 Zagreb
Croatia
+385-16041082
Finnish Lapland Film Commission
Valtakatu 21
96200 Rovaniemi
Finland
+358-408207575
Georgian National Film Commission
4. Z. Gamsakhurdia Sanapiro Street
0105 Tbilisi
Georgia
+995-322999200
Ile-de-France Film Commission
30, rue Saint Augustin
75002 Paris
France
+33-0156881288
Jamaica Film Commission
18 Trafalgar Road
Kingston 10
Jamaica
+1-8769787755
Kenya Film Commission
76417
Nairobi

Kenya
+254-733650068
Krakow Film Commission
Wygrana 2
30-311 Kraków
Poland
+48 (12) 354 2552
Lacustre Film Commission of the Araucania Region
(WajMapü), Film in Chile
Arturo Prat 880
4931837 Villarrica
Chile
+56-99933297
Lodz Film Commission
EC1 Lodz - City of Culture
1/3 Targowa Str.
90-022 Lodz
Poland
+48 (42) 233 5051
LOWER AUSTRIAN FILM COMMISSION (LAFC)
Department for Art and Culture, Office of the
Government of Lower Austria
Landhausplatz 1
3109 Sankt Poelten
Austria
+43-2742900513210
Macedonian Film Agency
8 Mart br.4
1000 Skopje
Macedonia
+389-23224100
Malta Film Commission
St. Rocco Street

KKR 9062 Kalkara
Malta
+356-21809135
Marrakesh Film Commission
Lot. Al Massar 2
Imtidad 178
40000 Marrakesh
Morocco
+212-661257326
Mauritius Film Development Corporation
Otter Barry Road
Floreal
Mauritius
+230-6963137
Mid Nordic Film Commission
PB 964 Sentrum
7410 Trondheim
Norway
+47-95488121
Namibia Film Commission
PO Box 40715
Ausspannplatz
Windhoek
Namibia
+264-61381900
Netherlands Film Commission
Pijnackerstraat 5
Noord Holland
1072 JS Amsterdam
Netherlands
+31-205707676
Oresund Film Commission - Sweden
Sixten Sparres gata 1

SE-271 39 Ystad
Sweden
+46-707163202
Ouarzazate Film Commission
Av Moulay Rachid-Batiment CRI/ 2nd Floor
45000 Ouarzazate
Morocco
Rotterdam Film Commission
Stationsplein 45
3013 AK Rotterdam
Netherlands
Netherlands
+31-104332511
Screen Brussels
Rue Royale 2-4
1000 Brussels
Belgium
+32-25480455
Screen Flanders
Flanders Film House
Bischoffsheimlaan 38
BE-1000 Brussels
Belgium
+32-2260630
Stockholm Film Commission
Greta Garbos vag 11
16940 Solna, Stockholm
Sweden
+46-708484621
Ticino Film Commission
Palazzo Marcacci
Casella Postale 20
6601 Locarno

Switzerland
+41-0917511975
Trinidad & Tobago Film Company Ltd. (FilmTT)
47 Long Circular Road
St James
Trinidad and Tobago
+1-8686281156
Valparaiso Film Commission
Melgarejo 669
9th Floor
Valparaiso
Chile
+56-322326029
Vienna Film Commission
Karl-Farkas-Gasse 18
1030 Vienna
Austria
+43-1400087000
Vilnius Film Office
Konstitucijos Av. 3-222
LT-09601 Vilnius
Lithuania
+370-61404696
West Finland Film Commission
Lantinen rantakatu 13
20100 Turku
Finland
+358-505590549
Western Norway Film Commission
Georgernes Verft 12
N-5011 Bergen
Norway
+47-55553642

Argentina Film Commission
Av. Belgrano 1586, 11th Floor
Buenos Aires
Argentina
+54-1143836933

Bahamas Film Commission
British Colonial Hilton-Corporate Office Center
One Bay Street
Nassau
Bahamas
+1-2423022000

Barcelona Film Commission
c/ Pujades, 81
08005 Barcelona
Spain
+34-934548066

Bath Film Office
Lewis House
Manvers Street
Bath
BA1 1LG
United Kingdom
+44 1225 477711

Belize Film Commission
69 Albert Street
Belize City
Belize
+501-6630110

British Film Commission
The Arts Building
Morris Place
London
N4 3JG

United Kingdom
+44 20 7613 7677
Busan Film Commission
52 Haeundae-haebyunro, haeundae-gu
612-824 Busan
South Korea
+82-517200301
Cardiff Film Office
Room CY1, City of Cardiff Council
County Hall, Atlantic Wharf, Cardiff Bay
Cardiff
CF10 4UW
United Kingdom
+44 29 2078 8562
Catalunya Film Commission
Passatge de la Banca, 1-3
08002 Barcelona
Spain
+34-935529163
Creative Scotland
The Lighthouse
11 Mitchell Lane
Glasgow
G1 3NU
United Kingdom
+44 141 302 1724
Dominican Republic Film Commission
Cayetano Rodriguez #154, Gascue
10205 Santo Domingo
Dominican Republic
+1-8096872166
Film Auckland
P.O. Box 147063

Ponsonby
Auckland -- 1144
New Zealand
+64-93650518
Film Fiji
Ground Floor, Civic House
New Town Hall Road,
Suva
Fiji
+679-3306662
Film London
The Tea Building, Suite 6.10
56 Shoreditch High Street
London
United Kingdom
+44 20 7613 7676
Film Madrid
Alcala, 31 - 1st Floor
28014 Madrid
Spain
+34-917208107
Film Otago Southland
Queenstown Lakes District Council
Private Bag 50072
Queenstown -- 9197
New Zealand
+64-274425268
Hagi Film Commission
The Tourism Division – Hagi City Office
510 Emukai
758-855 Hagi-shi Yamaguchi-ken
Japan
+81-838253139

Himeji Film Commission
Himeji City Tourism Promotion Department
68 Honmachi
670-0012 Himeji
Japan
+81-792873653
Hiroshima Film Commission
1-1 Nakajima-cho, Naka-ku
Hiroshima
Japan
+81-822476916
Huesca Film Office
Avenida Parque 3, 2-1E
22002 Huesca
Spain
+34-974101777
Illes Balears Film Commission
C/ Protectora 10
Palma
07012 Palma
Spain
+34-971177348
India Film Facilitation Office
National Film Development Corporation
Soochna Bhawan, Phase 1, CGO Complex, Lodhi Road
New Dehli 110 003
India
+91-1124367338
Irish Film Board
Queensgate
23 Dock Road
Galway
Ireland

+353-91561398
Kobe Film Office
c/o Kobe Convention & Visitors Association
6-9-1, Minatojima Nakamachi, Chuo-Ku
650-0046 Kobe
Japan
+81-783032021
Kyrgyz-Russian Independent Film Commission
37-92 Gastello Street
107014 Moscow
Russia
Liverpool Film Office
4th Floor Cunard Building
Pier Head, Water Street
Liverpool
L1 3ES
United Kingdom
+44 2623330178
Malaga Film Office
Plaza Jeses El Rico 5
29012 Malaga
Spain
+34-952601736
Mexican Film Commission
Insurgentes Sur #674, 2nd Floor
Col. del Valle
03100 Mexico City
Mexico
+52-5554485383
New Zealand Film Commission
Level 3; 119 Ghuznee Street
Wellington -- 6011
New Zealand

+64-43827680
Northern Ireland Screen
3rd Floor Alfred House
21 Alfred Street
Belfast
United Kingdom
+44 28 9023 2444
Panama Film Commission
Edison Plana, 3rd Floor
Ricardo J. Alfaro Avenue & El Paical
Panama City 01119
Panama
+507-5600638
Royal Film Commission of Jordan
PO Box 811991
Amman 11181
Jordan
+962-64642266
Screen Wellington
Level 1, 175 Victoria Street
Wellington -- 6021
New Zealand
+64-43820066
Segovia Film Office
Juderia Vieja 12
40001 Segovia
Spain
+34-921460354
Seoul Film Commission
1580 Sangam-dong, Mapo-gu
DMC Hi-Tech Industry Center 1F #114
03920 Seoul
South Korea

+82-27777184
Spain Film Commission
Calle Raso, 6, 1 Planta
41006 Sevilla
Spain
+34-954614009
Thailand Film Office
Department of Tourism
National Stadium, Rama 1 Road, Wangmai Pathumwan
Bangkok 10330
Thailand
+66-26124149
Tokyo Location Box
NISSHIN BLDG. 2F
346-6 Yamabukicho, Shinjuku-ku, Tokyo
162-0801 Tokyo
Japan
+81-355798464
Uruguay Film Commission
Juan Carlos Gomez 1276
11000 Montevideo
Uruguay
+598-29157469

A Coruna

Santiago de Compostela Film Commission
Rúa do Vilar, 63
15705 Santiago De Compostela A Coruna
Spain
+34-981580499

AB

Alberta Film
140 Whitemud Crossing
4211 - 106 Street
Edmonton, AB T6J 6L7
Canada
+1 (780) 422-8584
Calgary Film Commission
731 - 1 Street SE
Calgary, AB T2G 2G9
Canada

AL

Alabama Film Office
401 Adams Avenue, Suite 170
Montgomery, AL 36104
United States
Mobile Film Office, City of
164 St. Emanuel Street (36602)
P. O. Box 1827
Mobile, AL 36633
United States
+1 (251) 438-7100
Northeast Alabama Entertainment Initiative
1 O'Connell Street
Jacksonville, AL 36265
United States
+1 (256) 365-1640

AR

Little Rock Film Commission
400 W Capitol Ave., Ste 1700

Little Rock, AR 72201-3438
United States
+1 (501) 491-3418
Ozark-Franklin County Film Commission
300 West Commercial
Ozark, AR 72949
United States
+1 (479) 667-5337

AZ

Arizona Office of Film & Digital Media
118 No. 7th Avenue; Suite 400
Phoenix, AZ 85007
United States
+1 (602) 845-1296
Flagstaff Film Office
211 W. Aspen Ave.
Flagstaff, AZ 86001
United States
+1 (800) 217-2367*ext.* 2916
Page-Lake Powell Film Commission
PO Box 1180
Page, AZ 86040
United States
+1 (928) 645-4310
Phoenix Film Office, City of
200 W. Washington, 20th Floor
Phoenix, AZ 85003
United States
+1 (602) 262-4850
Tucson Film Office
Visit Tucson

100 South Church Avenue
Tucson, AZ 85701
United States
+1 (520) 770-2172

Balearic Islands

Mallorca Film Commission
Centre Cultural la Misericordia Placa de l'Hospital 4
07012 Palma de Mallorca Balearic Islands
Spain
+34-971219647

BC

Columbia Shuswap Film Commission
781 Marine Park Drive NE
P.O. Box 978
Salmon Arm, BC V1E 4P1
Canada
+1 (888) 248-2773
Creative BC
7 West 6th Avenue
Vancouver, BC V5Y 1K2
Canada
+1 (604) 730-2732
Thompson-Nicola Film Commission, BC
300 - 465 Victoria St.
Kamloops, BC V2C 2A9
Canada
+1 (250) 377-8673*ext.* 7058
Vancouver Film Commission
401 W. George Street; Ste 1500

Vancouver, BC V6B 5A1
Canada
+1 (604) 632-9668
Vancouver Island North Film Commission
#900 Alder Street
Campbell River, BC V9W 2P6
Canada
+1 (250) 287-2772

CA

Ausfilm
Ausfilm
2029 Century Park East, Suite 3150
Los Angeles, CA 90067
United States
+1 (310) 229-2362
Berkeley Film Office
2030 Addison St.
#102
Berkeley, CA 94704
United States
+1 (510) 549-7040
California Film Commission
7080 Hollywood Boulevard, Suite 900
Hollywood, CA 90028
United States
El Dorado Lake Tahoe Film & Media Office
542 Main Street
Placerville, CA 95667
United States
+1 (530) 626-4400
Film Oasis

Greater Palm Springs CVB
70100 Highway 111
Rancho Mirage, CA 92270
United States
+1 (760) 969-1360
Film Santa Barbara
500 E. Montecito Street
Santa Barbara, CA 93103
United States
+1 (805) 966-9222
FilmL.A.
6255 W. Sunset Blvd.
12th Floor
Los Angeles, CA 90028
United States
+1 (213) 977-8600
Fresno County Film Commission
2220 Tulare Street; Suite 800
Fresno, CA 93711
United States
+1 (559) 600-4271
Humboldt-Del Norte Film Commission
520 E Street
Eureka, CA 95501
United States
+1 (707) 443-4488
Huntington Beach Film Commission
301 Main Street, Suite 212
Huntington Beach, CA 92648
United States
+1 (714) 969-3492
Long Beach Office of Special Events & Filming
City Manager's Office / City of Long Beach

211 E. Ocean Blvd., Suite 410
Long Beach, CA 90802
United States
+1 (562) 570-5333
Marin Film Resource Office
1 Mitchell Blvd.; Ste B
San Rafael, CA 94903
United States
+1 (415) 925-2060
Monterey County Film Commission
PO Box 111
801 Lighthouse Avenue, Suite 104 (Zip Code: 93940)
Monterey, CA 93942
United States
+1 (831) 646-0910
Orange County Film Commission
53 La Costa Court
Laguna Beach, CA 92651
United States
+1 (949) 246-9704
Pasadena Film Office
100 No. Garfield Avenue
4th Floor
Pasadena, CA 91109
United States
+1 (626) 744-3964
Ridgecrest Regional Film Commission
643 N. China Lake Blvd. Suite C
PO Box 1838
Ridgecrest, CA 93555
United States
+1 (760) 375-8202
Riverside County Film Commission

3403 10th Street; Ste 400
Riverside, CA 92501
United States
+1 (951) 955-2044
Sacramento Film Commission
1608 I Street
Sacramento, CA 95814
United States
+1 (916) 808-5553
San Francisco Film Commission
City Hall, Room 473
One Dr. Carlton B. Goodlett Place
San Francisco, CA 94102
United States
+1 (415) 554-6241
San Luis Obispo County Film Commission
1334 March Street
San Luis Obispo, CA 93401
United States
+1 (805) 541-8000
San Mateo County Silicon Valley Film Commission
111 Anza Blvd., Suite #410
Burlingame, CA 94010
United States
+1 (650) 348-7600
Santa Clarita Film Office
23920 Valencia Boulevard, Suite 100
Santa Clarita, CA 91355-2175
United States
+1 (661) 284-1425
Santa Cruz County Film Commission
303 Water Street #100
Santa Cruz, CA 95060

United States
+1 (831) 425-1234*ext.* 112
Shasta County Film Commission
2334 Washington Avenue; Suite B
Redding, CA 96001
United States
+1 (530) 225-4103
Tulare County Film Commission
5961 S. Mooney Boulevard
Visalia, CA 93277
United States
+1 (559) 624-7187
Tuolumne County Film Commission
542 W Stockton Road
Sonora, CA 95370
United States
+1 (209) 533-4420

Canarias

Canary Islands Film
c/ Puerta Canseco, 49
Edificio Jamaica, 2ª
38003 Santa Cruz de Tenerife Canarias
Spain
+34-638765164

CO

Colorado Office of Film, Television, & Media
1625 Broadway, Ste. 2700
Denver, CO 80202
United States

+1 (303) 892-3840
Glenwood Springs Film Commission
P.O. Box 1238
Glenwood Springs, CO 81602
United States
+1 (970) 945-5002

CT

Connecticut Office of Film, Television and Digital Media
505 Hudson Street
Hartford, CT 06106
United States
+1 (860) 270-8198

DC

DC Office of Motion Picture & TV Development
1899 9th Street NE
Washington, DC 20018
United States
+1 (202) 671-0066

Durango

Durango, Mexico State Direction of Cinematography
Florida #1106 Barro del Calvario
34000 Durango
Mexico
+52-5522613158

FL

Bradenton Area Film

One Haben Blvd.
Palmetto, FL 34221
United States
+1 (941) 729-9177
Broward Office of Film, Music, Entertainment &
Creative Industries
101 NE Third Avenue; Suite 100
Fort Lauderdale, FL 33301
United States
+1 (954) 767-2467
Charlotte County Florida Film Office
18501 Murdock Circle, Suite 502
Port Charlotte, FL 33948
United States
Emerald Coast Film Commission
1540 Miracle Strip Pkwy
Fort Walton Beach, FL 32548
United States
+1 (850) 651-7644
Florida Office of Film and Entertainment
107 East Madison Street (MSC 80)
Tallahassee, FL 32399
United States
+1 (850) 717-8990
Miami Office of Film & Entertainment
444 SW 2nd Avenue
10th Floor
Miami, FL 33130
United States
+1 (305) 416-1072
Miami-Dade Office of Film & Entertainment
111 NW 1 Street, 12th Floor
Miami, FL 33128

United States
+1 (305) 375-3288
New Smyrna Beach Area CVB / Film Office
2238 SR 44
New Smyrna Beach, FL 32168
United States
+1 (386) 690-7111
Paradise Coast Film Commission
755 8th Avenue South
Naples, FL 34102
United States
+1 (239) 659-3456
Sarasota County Film & Entertainment Office
1680 Fruitville Road
Suite 402
Sarasota, FL 34236
United States
+1 (888) 765-5777*ext.* 104
St. Petersburg-Clearwater Area Film Commission
8200 Bryan Dairy Rd.
Suite 200
Largo, FL 33777
United States
+1 (727) 464-7240

GA

Atlanta Office of Film & Entertainment
55 Trinity Avenue SW; Ste 4350
Atlanta, GA 30303
United States
+1 (404) 330-6006
Clayton County Film Office

1588 Westwood Way
Morrow, GA 30260
United States
+1 (770) 477-4450
DeKalb County Film Commission
125 Clairemont Avenue; Suite 150
Dacatur, GA 30030
United States
+1 (404) 687-2748
Film Columbia County
1000 Business Blvd.
Evans, GA 30809
United States
+1 (706) 312-1375
Film Covington
2101 Clark Street
Covington, GA 30014
United States
+1 (920) 216-2393
Georgia Film, Music & Digital Entertainment Office
75 Fifth Street, NW, Suite 1200
Atlanta, GA 30312
United States
+1 (404) 962-4052
North Georgia Film, Inc.
465 Riley Road
Dahlonega, GA 30533
United States
+1 (706) 482-2707
Savannah Area Film Office
P.O. Box 128
Savannah, GA 31402
United States

+1 (912) 447-4159

HI

Hawaii Island Film Office
25 Aupuni Street, Room 1301
Hilo, HI 96720
United States
+1 (808) 961-8366
Hawaii State Film Office
250 S. Hotel St. Suite 510
Honolulu, HI 96813
United States
+1 (808) 586-2570
Honolulu Film Office/Island Of Oahu
530 S. King Street
Suite 306
Honolulu, HI 96813
United States
+1 (808) 768-6100
Kauai Film Commission
4444 Rice Street, Suite 200
Lihue, HI 96766
United States
+1 (808) 241-6386
Maui County Film Office
One Main Plaza
2200 Main St Ste 305
Wailuku, HI 96793
United States
+1 (808) 270-8237

Hong Kong

Create Hong Kong
40/F Revenue Tower
5 Gloucester Road Wanchai
Hong Kong Hong Kong
China
+852-25945745

IA

Produce Iowa
600 East Locust Street
Des Moines, IA 50319
United States
+1 (515) 725-0044

IL

Illinois Film Office
100 West Randolph
3rd Floor
Chicago, IL 60601
United States
+1 (312) 814-3600

IN

Film Indiana
1 North Capitol Avenue
Suite 600
Indianapolis, IN 46204
United States
+1 (317) 232-8897

Incheon

Icheon Film Commission
8F 68 Seokbawiro
Nam-gu Incheon
South Korea
+82-324557172

Jeonbuk

Jeonju Film Commission
125-14,Wonsangrim-gil
Wansan-gu
560-510 Jeonju-si Jeonbuk
South Korea
+82-632860421

KS

Wichita Film Commission
Go Wichita Convention & Visitor's Bureau
515 S Main Street, Suite 115
Wichita, KS 67202
United States
+1 (316) 265-2800

KwaZulu-Natal

KwaZulu-Natal Film Commission
115 Musgrave Road
10th Floor Musgrave Towers, Musgrave Centre
4001 Durban KwaZulu-Natal
South Africa
+27-313250200

KY

Kentucky Office of Film & Development
100 Airport Road, 2nd Floor
Frankfort, KY 40601
United States
+1 (800) 345-6591

LA

Baton Rouge Film Commission
359 Third Street
Baton Rouge, LA 70801
United States
+1 (225) 382-3562
Jefferson Louisiana Film Commission
1221 Elmwood Park Blvd., Suite 1002
Jefferson, LA 70123
United States
+1 (504) 736-6412
Lafayette Entertainment Initiative
705 West university Ave
Lafayette, LA 70502
United States
+1 (337) 291-3456
New Orleans Plantation Country
2900 Highway 51
Lalace, LA 70068
United States
+1 (985) 359-2562
Shreveport-Bossier Film Office
505 Travis Street
Shreveport, LA 71101
United States
+1 (318) 673-7515

West Baton Rouge Film Commission
2750 N. Westport Drive
Port Allen, LA 70767
United States
+1 (225) 332-2517

MA

Massachusetts Film Office
10 Park Plaza, Suite 4510
Boston, MA 02116
United States
+1 (617) 973-8400

MB

Manitoba Film & Music
410 - 93 Lombard Avenue
Winnipeg, MB R3B 3B1
Canada
+1 (204) 947-2040

MD

Baltimore Film Office
10 E. Baltimore Street
10th Floor
Baltimore, MD 21202
United States
+1 (410) 752-8632
Maryland Film Office
401 East Pratt Street, 14th Floor
Baltimore, MD 21202

United States
+1 (410) 767-6340

ME

Maine Film Office
59 State House Station
Augusta, ME 04333
United States
+1 (207) 624-9828

Mexico City

Mexico City Film Commission
Republica de Cuba, No. 41-43
Col. Centro, Del. Cuauhtemoc
06010 Mexico City
Mexico
+52-5517193012*ext.* 2071

MI

Michigan Film & Digital Media Office
300 N. Washington
Lansing, MI 48913
United States
+1 (800) 477-3456

MN

Minnesota Film and TV
401 North 3rd Street
Suite 245
Minneapolis, MN 55401-2316

United States
+1 (612) 767-0095

MO

KC Film Office
1321 Baltimore Street
Kansas City, MO 64105
United States
+1 (816) 691-3842
Missouri Film Commission
301 West High Street; 2nd Floor
Jefferson City, MO 65102
United States
+1 (573) 526-3566
Saint Louis Film Office
c/o St. Louis CVC
701 Convention Plaza, Ste 300
Saint Louis, MO 63101
United States
+1 (314) 992-0629

MS

Mississippi Film Office
P. O. Box 849
Jackson, MS 39205
United States
+1 (601) 359-3297
Tupelo Film Commission
399 East Main Street
P.O. Box 47
Tupelo, MS 38802-0047

United States
+1 (662) 841-6521

MT

Montana Film Office
301 S. Park Avenue
Helena, MT 59620
United States
+1 (406) 841-2876

NC

Charlotte Regional Film Commission
500 South College Street
Suite 300
Charlotte, NC 28202
United States
+1 (704) 331-2723
North Carolina Film Office
15000 Weston Parkway
Cary, NC 27513
United States
+1 (919) 447-7800
Piedmont Triad Film Commission
717 S. Marshall St., Suite 105-F
Winston-Salem, NC 27103
United States
+1 (336) 393-0001
Triangle Regional Film Commission
PO Box 13041
Research Triangle Park, NC 27709-3041
United States

+1 (919) 544-5501
Wilmington Regional Film Commission, Inc.
1223 North 23rd Street
Wilmington, NC 28405
United States
+1 (910) 343-3456

NE

Eastern Nebraska Film Office
302 South Woodland Court
Freemont, NE 68025
United States
+1 (402) 968-4280
Nebraska Film Office
Dept. of Economic Development
P.O. Box 94666
Lincoln, NE 68509-4666
United States
+1 (402) 471-3746

NH

New Hampshire Film and Television Office
19 Pillsbury St., 1st Floor
Concord, NH 03301
United States
+1 (603) 271-2220

NJ

Atlantic City Film Office
2314 Pacific Avenue

Atlantic City, NJ 08401
United States
+1 (609) 449-7151
New Jersey Motion Picture & TV Commission
153 Halsey Street
5th Floor
Newark, NJ 07101
United States
+1 (973) 648-6279

NL

Newfoundland & Labrador Film Development
Corporation
12 King's Bridge Road
St. John's, NL A1C 3K3
Canada
+1 (709) 738-3456

NM

Albuquerque Film Office
PO Box 1293
One Civic Plaza NW
Albuquerque, NM 87103
United States
+1 (505) 768-3283
Film Las Cruces
340 No. Reymond
Las Cruces, NM 88005
United States
+1 (575) 805-3456
New Mexico State Film Office

Joseph M. Montoya Building
1100 S. St. Francis Drive, Suite 1213
Santa Fe, NM 87505
United States
+1 (505) 476-5604
Otero County Film Office
1301 N. White Sands Blvd.
Alamogordo, NM 88310
United States
+1 (575) 439-4353
Santa Fe Film Office
102 Grant Avenue
Santa Fe, NM 87501
United States
+1 (505) 986-6293

NT

Northwest Territories Film Commission
Scotia Centre - 9th Floor
Box 1320
Yellowknife, NT X1A 2L9
Canada
+1 (844) 698-9456

NV

Nevada Film Office
6655 West Sahara Avenue
Suite C-106
Las Vegas, NV 89146
United States
+1 (702) 486-2711

NY

Bermuda Tourism Authority
675 Third Ave 20th Floor
New York, NY 10035
United States
+1 (212) 818-9800
Buffalo Niagara Film Office
Horizons Plaza
140 Lower Terrace
Buffalo, NY 14202
United States
+1 (716) 845-2200
Central New York / Onondaga County Film Commission
333 West Washington Street
Suite 130
Syracuse, NY 13202
United States
+1 (315) 435-3770
Nassau County Office of Cinema/TV Promotion
Executive Building
One West Street
Mineola, NY 11501
United States
+1 (516) 571-3168
New York State Governor's Office for Motion Picture &
TV Development
633 Third Ave.
33rd Floor
New York, NY 10017
United States
+1 (212) 803-2330
Rochester/Finger Lakes Film & Video Office, Inc.

45 East Avenue, Suite 400
Rochester, NY 14604-2294
United States
+1 (585) 279-8308

OH

FilmDayton
22 E. Fifth Street
Dayton, OH 45402
United States
+1 (937) 554-0031
Greater Cleveland Film Commission
1333 Lakeside Avenue E
Cleveland, OH 44114
United States
+1 (216) 623-3910*ext.* 1
Greater Columbus Film Commission
100 E. Broad Street
Suite 2250
Columbus, OH 43215
United States
+1 (614) 221-8648

OK

Oklahoma Film + Music Office
701 W. Sheridan Ave.
Oklahoma City, OK 73102
United States
+1 (800) 766-3456
Tulsa Office of Film, Music, Arts & Culture
1 W. Third Street

Suite 100
Tulsa, OK 74103
United States
+1 (918) 560-0286

ON

Brampton Film Office
2 Wellington Street West
Brampton, ON L6Y 4R2
Canada
+1 (905) 874-3361
Durham Regional Film Office
P.O. Box 623
605 Rossland Road East
Whitby, ON L1N 6A3
Canada
+1 (905) 668-4113*ext.* 2617
Mississauga Film Office
201 City Centre Drive
Suite 202
Mississauga, ON L5B 2T4
Canada
+1 (605) 306-6150
Ontario Media Development Corporation
175 Bloor St. East,
South Tower, Suite 501
Toronto, ON M4W 3R8
Canada
+1 (416) 314-6858
Toronto Film and Television Office
Toronto City Hall, Main Floor, West 1
100 Queen Street West

Toronto, ON M5H 2N2
Canada

PA

Greater Erie Film Office
1926 Peach Street
Suite 100
Erie, PA 16502
United States
+1 (814) 580-6608
Pittsburgh Film Office
Century Building
130 7th Street, Suite 202
Pittsburgh, PA 15222
United States
+1 (412) 261-2744

QC

Quebec Film & Television Council
204 Saint-Sacrement Street, Suite 500
Montreal, QC H2Y 1W8
Canada
+1 (514) 499-7070

QLD

Screen Queensland
Suite 1, 30 Florence St
Newstead
Brisbane QLD 4006
Australia

+61 732480500

RJ

Rio Film Commission
Rua das Laranjeiras, 307
Rio de Janeiro - Rio de Janeiro
22240-004
Brazil
+55-2122257082*ext.* 259

RM

Film Commission Roma & Lazio
Via Tuscolana 1055
00173 Roma RM
Italy
+39-06722863200
Italian Film Commission (Italian Trade Agency)
Via Liszt 21
00144 Roma RM
Italy
+1 (323) 879-0950

Salamanca

Salamanca Film Commission
Plaza Mayor, n°19,1°
37002 Salamanca
Spain
+34-923272408

SC

South Carolina Film Commission
1205 Pendleton Street
Room 225
Columbia, SC 29201
United States
+1 (803) 737-0490

SD

South Dakota Film Commission
711 East Wells Avenue
Pierre, SD 57501
United States

Sevilla

Carmona Film Office
Ayuntamiento de Carmona\nAlcazar de la Puerta Sevilla,
s/n
41410 Carmona Sevilla
Spain

South Africa

Cape Film Commission
Westlake Square - Unit A3
Westlake Drive Westlake
7945 Cape Town South Africa
South Africa
+27-217010924

SP

São Paulo City Film Commission

Avenida São João, 473 - 7º andar
São Paulo - São Paulo
01035-000
Brazil
+55-1132248124

Surrey

Surrey Film Office
County Hall
Penrhyn Road
Kingston-Upon-Thames
Surrey
KT1 2DN
United Kingdom
+44 20 8213 2737

TN

Memphis & Shelby County Film & Television
Commission
50 Peabody Place, Suite 250
Memphis, TN 38103
United States
+1 (901) 527-8300
Tennessee Film, Ent & Music
312 Rosa L. Parks Avenue, 26th Floor
Nashville, TN 37243
United States
+1 (615) 741-3456

TX

Austin Film Commission
111 Congress Ave
Ste 700
Austin, TX 78701
United States
+1 (512) 583-7230
Brownsville Border Film Commission
1034 E. Levee Street
2nd Floor
Brownsville, TX 78520
United States
+1 (956) 548-6150
Corpus Christi Convention & Visitors Bureau
101 No. Shoreline Blvd
Ste. 430
Corpus Christi, TX 78401-2825
United States
+1 (361) 881-1810
Dallas Film Commission
Dallas City Hall
1500 Marilla St., 2C North
Dallas, TX 75201
United States
+1 (214) 671-9821
El Paso Film Commission
#1 Civic Center Plaza
El Paso, TX 79901
United States
+1 (915) 534-0698
Fort Worth Film Commission
111 W. 4th Street
Suite 200
Fort Worth, TX 76102

United States
+1 (817) 698-7842
Houston Film Commission
701 Avenida de las Americas, Suite 200
Houston, TX 77010
United States
+1 (713) 853-8956
Rio Grande Valley Film Commission
1200 Ash Ave.
McAllen, TX 78501
United States
+1 (956) 682-2871
San Antonio Film Commission
115 Plaza de Armas
Suite 102
San Antonio, TX 78205
United States
+1 (210) 207-6777
Texas Film Commission
P.O. Box 12428
Austin, TX 78711
United States
+1 (512) 463-9200

UT

Kanab/Kane County Film Commission
78 South 100 East
Kanab, UT 84741
United States
+1 (435) 644-5033
Moab To Monument Valley Film Commission
111 East 100 North

Moab, UT 84532
United States
+1 (435) 259-4341
Park City Film Commission
1850 Sidewinder Drive, #320
P.O. Box 1630
Park City, UT 84060
United States
+1 (435) 658-9622
Utah Film Commission
300 North State Street
Salt Lake City, UT 84114
United States
+1 (800) 453-8824

VA

Martinsville-Henry County Film Office
191 Fayette Street, Third Floor (24112)
Martinsville, VA 24114-0631
United States
+1 (276) 632-8006
Virginia Film Office
901 East Cary Street, Ste 9000
Richmond, VA 23219
United States
+1 (800) 854-6233

VI

U.S. Virgin Islands Film Office
PO Box 6400
St. Thomas VI 00804

U.S. Virgin Islands
+1 (340) 774-8784*ext.* 2243

VIC

Film Victoria
Level 3, 55 Collins Street
GPO Box 4361
Melbourne VIC 3000
Australia
+61 3 9660 3215

West Midlands

Film Birmingham
Library of Birmingham
Broad Street
Birmingham
West Midlands
B1 2ND
United Kingdom
+44 121 675 3883

WV

West Virginia Film Office
90 MacCorkle Avenue, SW
South Charleston, WV 25303
United States
+1 (866) 698-3456

WY

Film Wyoming

5611 High Plains Road
Cheyenne, WY 82007
United States
+1 (307) 777-3400

YT

Yukon Media Development
P.O. Box 2703 (F3)
Whitehorse, YT Y1A 2C6
Canada
+1 (867) 667-5400